The Execution of Sheriffs' Warrants

2nd Edition

J.A. Keith, FCA, W.B. Podevin
& Claire Sandbrook, LL.B.

Barry Rose Law Publishers Ltd
Chichester, England

THE EXECUTION OF

SHERIFFS' WARRANTS

2ND EDITION

by

J.A. KEITH, FCA, W.B. PODEVIN & CLAIRE SANDBROOK, LL.B.

Lately Officers to the Sheriffs of Greater London, Surrey,
Hertfordshire & Leicestershire, Serjeant at Mace
to the Sheriffs of the City of London.
Solicitor of the Supreme Court & Deputy Sheriff
of Greater London

"It is indeed, somewhat surprising that any person can be found to undertake an office involving such onerous and responsible duties, and were it not for the dignity which attaches to one of the most ancient and honourable of public offices, the post might well go begging."

(*The Law Times* of May 14, 1898
on Sheriffs and their problems).

Printing History

First edition published by the Sheriffs' Officers' Association of England & Wales 1988

This edition ISBN 1 872328 34 2

Published by

Barry Rose Law Publishers Ltd
Chichester
West Sussex

© Copyright J.A. Keith, W.B. Podevin, Barry Rose Law Publishers Ltd 1996

Preface
to the First Edition

There are a number of volumes on the subject of Execution intended for members of the legal profession but none available which could be described as a "Practical Guide" for the active Sheriff's Officer and his staff.

In 1901, the Sheriffs' Officers' Association published the Red Book, which was a collection of notes on decided cases in connection with the law of Sheriff. That volume was of considerable use to Officers and was maintained by means of paste-in slips issued by the Association as new cases arose. However, it became obsolete many years ago and was discontinued.

The present work is not intended to be a replacement for the Red Book although some of our material is drawn from that source. We intend that this, while not a textbook, be an aid to the practising Officer and to that end contains notes of the Authorities. Some blank pages are inserted in the text for personal notes and references (as had the original work). The law is stated as at December 1987.

As this volume is a guide only, no responsibility is undertaken for any damages which may arise as a result of following the advice given. It is for the individual Sheriff's Officer to ensure that he conducts himself professionally, diligently, impartially and correctly at all times.

We are grateful to our friends and associates who have assisted in the preparation of the book, particularly to Alastair Black, DL, Malcolm Butler, MA, LL.B, Sylvia Keith, BA and William C.Podevin.

JAK & WBP
January 1988

Preface
to the Second Edition

Some eight years have elapsed since the first edition was published by The Sheriffs' Officers' Association of England and Wales. In those years, the book found favour, not only with Officers but also with solicitors and accountants who found it convenient to have to hand, an aide memoire to enforcement by the Sheriff's Office.

In undertaking the revision we have sought to include notes on all aspects of the modern practice of the Sheriffs and Under Sheriffs. New chapters have been added and others, particularly those on Insolvency and Interpleader have been completely re-written.

The original authors were delighted to welcome to the 'editorial team', Claire Sandbrook, a solicitor of the Supreme Court, Deputy Sheriff of Greater London and a partner in the firm of Burchell and Ruston. Her contribution has been considerable and much appreciated.

We wish also to express our appreciation of those colleagues who assisted us with the first edition, some again with the second, and also to our new publisher's staff who have been so helpful and patient in the preparation of this new edition.

The law is stated as at June 1995.

JAK, WBP, CS.
December 1995

CONTENTS

Table of Statutes

Statutory Instruments

Court Rules

Table of Cases

Bibliography

MATHER ON SHERIFF AND EXECUTION LAW
    3rd Edition, 1935
    Published by Stevens & Sons Ltd & Sweet & Maxwell Ltd.

THE SUPREME COURT PRACTICE
    1993 and 1995
    Published by Stevens & Sons Ltd & Sweet & Maxwell Ltd.

THE COUNTY COURT PRACTICE 1994
    Published by Butterworth & Co. (Publishers) Ltd.

HALSBURY'S LAWS OF ENGLAND
    4th Edition
    Published by Butterworth & Co. (Publishers) Ltd.

ENFORCEMENT OF A JUDGMENT
    8th Edition, 1992, by Alastair Black, D.L. & Duncan Black
    Published by Longman Group Ltd.

RYDE ON RATING
    13th Edition, (3rd Supp), 1983.
    by G.R.G. Roots & N.G.A. King
    Published by Butterworth & Co. (Publishers) Ltd.

BUTTERWORTHS INSOLVENCY LAW HANDBOOK
    1994 by M. Crystal, QC
    Published by Butterworth & Co (Publishers) Ltd.

CHAPTER 1

The Office of Sheriff

The Sheriff occupies the earliest secular office in the country other than that of the Kingship, being traceable to early Saxon times. By the 10th century, the power of the Sheriff had grown and he had become the principal officer of the Crown within his county. He was responsible for the administration of the criminal law, raising "hue and cry" if necessary, for the collection of the King's revenue and for the maintenance of the King's peace. He also had some judicial functions. He held office only during the King's pleasure.

William I (the Conqueror) realised that the institution of the Shrievalty could be used to balance and subsequently diminish the great power of the nobles and barons and instigated a gradual transfer of power which left the Sheriff supreme in the Shires and in control of all the Shire administration. Twice yearly, at Easter and Michaelmas, each Sheriff was obliged to appear at the Exchequer to account for the taxes raised. The penalty for latecoming was severe - a fine of £5 for each day represented an exemplary punishment.

Although by the 13th century a central bureaucracy had been established, the duties of the Sheriff continued to increase with the growing sophistication of the civil and judicial administration in the country. By the end of that century, the Sheriffs had achieved a position of great power and influence.

Inevitably, there was corruption and misuse of that power. Steps were taken to reduce the field of influence by removing some responsibilities to new appointments. The post of High Constable was created to have care of the Army (but not for the supply of arms which remained with the Sheriff). In 1557 this authority was again transferred to the Lord Lieutenant who combined military duties with judicial as Chief Magistrate.

In later times, various statutes were passed to limit the Shrieval power. The tour of office was limited to one year. Often the Crown had difficulty in finding subjects who were willing to undertake the arduous and frequently expensive requirements of the office and found it necessary to make refusal of the office an offence.

In the 19th century, the Office was restructured and codified anew in the Sheriffs Acts of 1837 and 1887. The earlier difficulties the Sheriff had experienced with the Exchequer were relieved and the appointment brought up to date.

The Sheriff is still the principal executive officer of the Crown within his Shrievalty despite a further diminution of his duties in recent years. He is the officer charged with the execution of most of the judgments and orders of the High Court. His responsibility for the execution of death penalties, when imposed by the Queen's Justices, was abolished by the Courts Act, 1971 but could be re-instated should capital punishment be re-introduced. He may, in extension of his power, call upon the *posse comitatus*, or power of the Shire, to aid him in the execution of his duties or indeed as a last resort in the defence of his County.

(For further reading, see *Mather on Sheriff & Execution Law*, 3rd edn, ch.1; *The Sheriff-The Man and his Office*,

Irene Gladwin, Gollancz, 1974.)

APPOINTMENT

By s.3 of the Sheriffs Act, 1887, a Sheriff shall be appointed for each county to hold office for no more than one year. The appointee is required "to have sufficient land within his county or bailiwick to answer the Queen and her people." "A person who has been sheriff of a county for a whole year shall not within three years next ensuing be appointed sheriff of that county unless there is no other person in the county qualified to fill the office" (*ibid.*, s.5).

It would be impractical to expect that a Sheriff, appointed for one year only, could within that time acquire sufficient expertise to be able to undertake the complex processes involved in the execution of High Court judgments. He is therefore enjoined by Statute to appoint an Under Sheriff and sufficient Officers to carry out his duties.

By s.23 of the Act, the Sheriff shall "within one month after the notification of his appointment in the London Gazette ... appoint some fit person to be his Under Sheriff ...".

To ensure continuity within the office it is usual for the Sheriff to appoint an Under Sheriff who is experienced and likewise Officers who are similarly expert. However, there is no compulsion for the Sheriff to appoint either the Under Sheriff or the Officers of his predecessor.

While it is customary for the Under Sheriff to perform the duties of the Sheriff, unless the actual presence of the Sheriff is necessary, the Under Sheriff is only to a certain extent recognized by the Law. The Law holds the Sheriff responsible for all acts done or omitted to be done by his

Under Sheriff. It is usual for the Under Sheriff to be a solicitor but this is not a requirement under the statute.

Each Sheriff, except in the cases of the Shrievalties of the City of London and the county of Greater London who already maintain such offices, also appoints a London deputy or agent, usually a member of a firm of solicitors, to maintain an office within one mile of Inner Temple Hall for the receipt of writs, rules and orders in connexion with process directed to the Sheriff (s.24 *ibid.*). Delivery of a writ to the deputy in London is delivery to the Sheriff (*Woodland v. Fuller* (1840) 3 P & D 570).

Officers and Bailiffs are appointed by the Sheriff. There is no particular form of appointment, although those appointed are required to make a declaration (an example is given at the end of this chapter) that they will not misuse or sell their office (s.26 *ibid.*). The term "bailiff" appears to be interchangeable with that of Sheriff's Officer or Serjeant at Mace. A Bailiff or Officer is not permitted to appoint a deputy (*Jackson v. Hill* (1839) 10 A & E 484).

A Sheriff's Officer may not be a minor as the position is one of responsibility and trust (*Cuckson v. Winter* (1828) 2 M & R 317).

By s.9(1)(a) Licensing Act 1964, a Sheriff's Officer may not hold a licence for the sale of intoxicating liquor.

The appointment as Sheriff's Officer is not a contract of service. The relationship of master and servant does not exist between Sheriff and Officer (*In re High Sheriff of Hertfordshire, in re De Jones* (1928) WN 269).

In the past it was usual for the Sheriff to seek an indemnity from his Officer, hence the expression "bound bailiff" or in degenerative form "bum bailiff", but modern commercial practice has encouraged the use of professional indemnity insurance instead. All insurance policies of this type should include the Sheriff as one of the insured as any action for negligence, or for failure to perform a duty, should be brought against the Sheriff and not against the Officer, (*Anon* (1772) Loft 81 and see *Mather*, 3rd edn, p.43).

The need for registration under the Consumer Credit Act, 1974 was the subject of correspondence with the Office of Fair Trading in March 1976. Their view is:

"That a person appointed to office as Sheriff does not need a licence under the Consumer Credit Act to carry out the functions derived from such appointment. Nor do we think anyone assisting the Sheriff to carry out his functions will require a licence. Nor do we consider that properly appointed bailiffs require a licence to deal with matters arising by virtue of their appointment.

"People such as auctioneers, removal contractors and so on employed as agents during the execution of warrants do not, in our view, require a licence on that account."

"Special Bailiff" is a term applied to one appointed by a Sheriff at the express request of a creditor and whose authority holds good for the execution of a single and particular warrant alone. This practice may be used where an execution is of a highly specialised nature. The Sheriff, in such cases, appears to be absolved from all responsibility for the execution and indeed is not required to rule a return to such a writ (*Harding v. Holder* (1841) 9DPC 659). A simple request from a judgment creditor that a particular Officer have conduct of a matter is not a request for appointment as a special bailiff (*Corbet v. Brown* (1838) 6 DPC 794; *Balson v. Meggat* (1836) 4 Dawl 557).

There is no prescribed form of identification or warrant card used by Sheriff's Officers or Bailiffs but in most counties a document signed by the Under Sheriff showing the name and bearing a photograph of the Officer is used. The Sheriffs' Officers' Association promote a scheme whereby Officers who are members of the Association, and their associated staffs, may carry an identification badge bearing their name, photograph and the Association badge to assist in the proper identification of Officers to the public.

The High Sheriff, and following from his authority, the Under Sheriff and Sheriff's Officers, are required to obey the terms of any writ delivered to the office for execution and are bound to observe any lawful instructions given to them concerning the execution of the writ. However, the Sheriff is not, in normal circumstances, the agent of the party putting him into motion. Not only does the Sheriff have a duty towards the judgment creditor but he also has duties towards the judgment debtor.

Following the administrative re-organization of 1974, legislated in the Local Government Act 1972, many new shrievalties were formed and old ones dismantled. However the Lord Chancellor prescribed by SI 1974/222 that the bailiwicks of the Under Sheriffs, with the exception of Glamorgan, should continue as they were prior to April 1, 1974. Where administrative boundaries have changed since that time, shrievalty boundaries have generally followed the administrative, but writs are lodged with, and dealt with, by the Under Sheriffs and Officers who previously had responsibility for those areas. Bailiwicks therefore follow the 'old' county maps of England and Wales.

Certain ancient cities and towns have retained their Sheriffs despite the re-organizations, for example the Borough and Town of Berwick-upon-Tweed, City of Canterbury, City of London, Cities of Newcastle-upon-Tyne, Norwich, Worcester and York amongst others, and writs are still directed to the Sheriffs of those cities and counties. For a full list and proper forms of direction see the Supreme Court Practice, 1993, vol.2, part 3, at para.923.

(For further reference, see Sheriff's Act 1887; *Mather*, ch.3 and *Halsbury's Laws of England*, "Sheriffs & Bailiffs".)

OFFICE STRUCTURE

As the office of the Sheriff has evolved over the centuries there are local variations as to procedures and office organization. Nevertheless, the basic structure is common to all insofar as the Sheriff has the final responsibility for the conduct of his office. The Under Sheriff represents the Sheriff in most day to day activities, deals with receipt of writs, issuing warrants and so on in addition usually to acting as the Sheriff's solicitor. The Sheriff's Officer's duty is that of attending and reporting on the warrants issued to him.

In the busier counties, the Officers are normally full time, self employed, and members of firms which have existed for many years. Indeed, some can trace their history for 150 years or more.

In the counties with less volume of business there may still be a long history of continuity but the Officers may also practice in another profession such as auctioneering or estate agency. They are able to bring the expertise they have gained in those professions to that gained as Officers. In some counties, the Officer may be a direct employee of the Under Sheriff and answerable to him as a member of his staff.

Similarly, there are Under Sheriffs whose practices can be traced back to the latter part of the 18th century; there are Under Sheriffs who devote most of their time to the work of the Shrievalty and there are those who devote most of their time to their solicitors' practices.

As a result, the duty of reporting and accounting to execution creditors varies from being entirely that of the Under Sheriff to being entirely that of the Sheriff's Officers.

However, whosoever has the duty, the pyramid of responsibility does not vary. At the head is the Sheriff, to whom all his appointees are accountable and who may dismiss, at will, Under Sheriff or Officer or Bailiff without notice and without compensation. He can insist, on threat of dismissal, on recompense being made to an aggrieved party.

The advantage of this structure is that any party has access to one who has responsibility for the actions of an offending official. Should any complaint be unsatisfied there remains a right of action against the Sheriff personally.

In the present volume the term "Sheriff" is to be understood to include the whole of the official structure of the office except where a duty falls to be executed by the Sheriff in person.

Example of the Declaration to be sworn by the Sheriff's Officer

I_____of_____

do solemnly and sincerely declare that I will not use or exercise the Office of Sheriff's Officer corruptly during the time that I shall remain therein neither shall nor will accept receive or take by any colour means or device whatsoever or consent to the taking of any manner of fee or reward of any person or persons before the returning of any tales in any Court of Record of the Queen or betwixt party & party above such fees as are allowed for the same by law but will according to my power truly and indifferently with convenient speed return all such writs touching the same as shall appertain to be done by my duty or office during the time I shall remain in the said office.

_____ Signature

Declared before me at_____

this _____ day of_____19_____

_____

A Justice of the Peace for_____

CHAPTER 2

Writs Generally

Types of Writ

The Sheriff deals with the enforcement of all High Court writs including those transferred for execution to the High Court from the County Court and with warrants issued under the provisions of the Lands Clauses Acts. These writs are dealt with more particularly hereafter but are listed below.

1. Writ of *fieri facias*
2. Writ of Possession & *fieri facias*
3. Writ of Possession
4. Writ of Delivery
5. Writ of Restitution
6. Writ of Assistance
7. Writ of *ne exeat regno*
8. Warrant under Compulsory Purchase Order (Lands Clauses)

Note that the last mentioned is issued as a step in an administrative process and is not a judicial writ.

Lodgment of Writ

The writ must be delivered to the Sheriff, Under Sheriff

or London Agent for execution; it may not be delivered to the Sheriff's Officer as it is no part of the latter's duty to receive writs and the Sheriff is not liable if the writ is not properly executed (*Triminger v. Keen* (1882) WN 106). Delivery to the London Agent is equivalent to lodgment with the Under Sheriff.

If the Sheriff is a party to the writ, it must be directed to the Coroner as the Sheriff may not levy on his own behalf. Where the Coroner is also a party, the writ will be directed to persons appointed by the court known as elisors. Section 15, Coroners Act 1887 (repealed and replaced by the Coroners Act 1988) provided that the Coroners were entitled to receive the same poundage, fees or other compensation as the Sheriff for the execution of a writ and the Coroner was liable to the same penalties in cases of misconduct or negligence. (See also *Halsbury* 4th edn, vol.9, at para.1038 *et seq.*)

Life of the Writ

The life of a writ is generally one year commencing from its date of teste and may be extended or renewed if it is not completed in that time. Where interpleader proceedings are instituted, expiry is automatically extended to the day 12 months after the conclusion of those proceedings. To retain priority the writ must be renewed before expiry. A writ which is renewed after expiry takes priority from its renewal date only, (RSC, O.46, r.8).

Where a Writ of Possession and *fi:fa* is issued, the expiry date may be determined by applying the separate rules for the expiry of the two parts; that is, the *fi:fa* may expire at a later time than the writ of possession if interpleader ensues.

The exception to these rules concerns a Writ of Assistance which does not expire by the passage of time. The writ is usually directed to the "Present and Future Sheriffs of ...". A warrant issued to enforce a Compulsory Purchase Order does not expire, O.46 concerns judicial writs only.

No action should be taken by the Sheriff in anticipation of lodgment before the writ is lodged with either the Under Sheriff or his London Agent, or after the writ has expired, as the Sheriff has no authority to act except upon a valid writ lodged with him.

Timing the Writ

It is obligatory for the Sheriff to record the date and time of receipt of the writ to establish the priority as against others he may receive and against others that may be lodged in the County Court (s.138(3), Supreme Court Act 1981). This is referred to in more detail under the heading PRIORITY.

Effect of the Writ

From the time of lodgment of the writ the goods of the debtor are bound in his hands; the judgment debtor is prevented from disposing of his assets other than for valuable consideration to a purchaser in good faith who has had no notice of the writ (s.138(1), Supreme Court Act, 1981).

The Content of the Writ

The writ is in several parts: first the title and greeting;

secondly, a resume of the judgment; thirdly, the command as to what is to be levied or delivered; fourthly, the witness (the Lord Chancellor or President of the Family Division); and lastly, the endorsement, which does not form part of the writ proper, showing details of the parties' addresses (see RSC, O.45, r.1. & Appendix A, *Supreme Court Practice*, vol.2, part 2, Prescribed Forms, form 53 *et seq*).

Additional instructions may be given by letter attached to the writ but these do not form part of the writ and may not seek to increase the amount of any levy.

Certain writs may not permit the levy of charges or costs. These must be noted with care, as to seek those charges from a debtor would constitute an excessive levy. Credits received after the issue of the writ should be advised to the Sheriff by the instructing solicitor and must be carefully noted for the same reason.

As the writ is the document from which the Sheriff and thus the Officer derives the authority to seize or to sell, it is essential that the original be examined with care to ensure all is correctly stated, that totals tally, that dates agree and so on. The authority of the Sheriff is restricted to the Command in the writ. The Sheriff may take no action towards the execution until the original sealed writ is in his hands. A copy of the writ transmitted to the Under Sheriff by fax is insufficient for execution to commence.

If, on the face of it, the Order contained in the writ is not clearly outside the jurisdiction of the Court making it, the Sheriff will be protected when he acts in obedience to it (*The Marshalsea* (1613) 10 Co.Rep 76A) but we suggest that the Sheriff may be held liable if action is taken by him upon a writ that is patently incorrect.

Time of Execution

A writ or process may not be executed on any Sunday of the year unless an order of the Court is made permitting such execution. A writ may not be executed on Good Friday nor on Christmas Day, which days appear to count as legal Sundays (RSC, O.65, r.10 following s.6, 29 Car II c.7).

THE WARRANT

The warrant is a translation of the command in the writ addressed to the Sheriff into a command from the Sheriff to his Officer. The warrant will set out the following:

1. To whom the warrant is directed.
2. The title of the action, who is plaintiff and who is defendant.
3. The date of teste of the writ.
4. The name of the party against whom the writ is to be enforced.
5. How much is to be levied with brief details of the division between debt and costs, or what is to be seized or delivered.
6. The interest rates and dates if any.
7. A caution that the result is to be reported to the Sheriff.
8. A summary of the command.
9. An endorsement stating the name and address of the issuing solicitors.
10. An endorsement stating the address of the debtor.
11. A caution that the goods of an ambassador are exempt from seizure.

The warrant is sealed by the Sheriff and bears his name and date of issue. The warrant is thus directed to named Officers and is a command from the Sheriff of the County to, in the case of a writ of *fi:fa*, "make of the goods and chattels" of the debtor the sum owing, and is also an authority to levy costs and expenses in accordance with the Sheriff's Scale of Fees.

PRIORITY OF WRITS

Monies received from debtors must be applied to writs in the strict order of priority established by the actual time and date of lodgment with the Under Sheriff or the London Deputy, or with the District Judge (formerly the Registrar).

A writ which has been renewed or extended has priority from the date and time of the original lodgment provided that the renewal or extension is sought before the expiry of the writ (RSC, O.46, r.8).

Judgment Set Aside

A writ which is withdrawn after judgment, is set aside and then re-instated following an appeal, will take as its priority the date of the original lodgment. However if goods have been sold in the interim, the later creditor, being the one on whose behalf the sale took place, will retain the proceeds of the sale (*Bankers Trust v. Galadari* (1986) 3 All ER 794).

Several Writs

If a solicitor acting for several plaintiffs lodges several

writs simultaneously then they may enjoy equal priority. The Sheriff is not entitled to insist that they be lodged in any specific order and a return that he had received them simultaneously and levied under all is good (*Ashworth v. Earl of Uxbridge* (1842) 12 LJ(NS) QB 39). If two writs are lodged on different days and no sale has taken place, the first has priority notwithstanding that the second was levied first (*Hutchinson v. Johnson* (1787) 1 TR 729), and the rule was clearly stated in *Wells v. Croft* (1893) 68 LT 231:

> "If two writs against the same person are delivered to the Sheriff, he must execute that first which was delivered, even though both were delivered on the same day. That is to say, he must apply the proceeds of sale under them in satisfaction of that writ which was first delivered to him, for when the Sheriff seizes the goods, they are, in point of law, in his custody under all the writs which he then has and when he sells, he does so, in point of law, under all such writs.
>
> "If the Sheriff, when the second writ is delivered to him, has seized goods under the first, he may be said, immediately upon delivery of the latter writ, to have seized the goods under that also."

Fraudulent Judgment

If goods are seized under a fraudulent judgment, the Sheriff is obliged to sell under a later and genuine writ, provided he has notice of the fraud (*Christopherson v. Burton* (1848) 18 LJ Ex 60).

Suspended Writs

Where a writ of *fi:fa* is lodged but the Sheriff is asked to suspend action, he must levy under a later writ in preference to the earlier (*Kempland v. Macauley* (1791) 1 Peake 95; *Crowder v. Long* (1828) 8 B & C 598; *Hunt v. Hooper* (1844) 13 LJ Ex 183; and see also *Mather*, 3rd edn, at p.81).

Crown Priority

At common law, the priority of the Crown in execution commences from the time that the debt becomes a debt of record. This was recognized in the statute 33 Henry 8, c.39. (See also *Rex v. Stoper* (1818) 6 Price 114, *Butler v. Butler* (1801) 1 East 338.) In general, the title of the Crown will attach from the date of teste of the writ. Also in this connexion see s.5, Crown Suits Act 1865 and the more modern Crown Proceedings Act 1947. Section 26(1) of the last mentioned referred to the manner of enforcement of Crown writs but did not alter the prerogative of the Crown to take priority over a subject. An execution issued by the Crown takes precedence provided that the goods have not been sold (see *The County Court Practice 1994, Part 1*, at p.80). For a full list of the Government departments which are recognized as departments of the Crown and entitled to priority see *The County Court Practice 1994*, at p.852. These include, as one would expect, the Inland Revenue, Customs & Excise, DSS and the Crown Estate Commissioners, but there are many others in addition.

County Court Priority

Priority of County Court warrants is established by reference to the time and date of lodgment or issue of the process. The Sheriff must record the date and time of lodgment and the District Judge must do likewise (s.138(3), Supreme Court Act, 1981, and the corollary s.85, County Court Act, 1984).

Both Sheriff and District Judge have an obligation to declare to the other the date and time of their own writ or warrant, (s.104, County Court Act 1984).

A County Court warrant forwarded to a "foreign court" takes priority from the date and time it is received at the enforcing Court.

THE COUNTY COURT & TRANSFER OF WRITS

Transfer of Warrants between County Court and Sheriff

Agreement was reached with the Lord Chancellor's Department as to procedures to be followed when the County Court Bailiff found that the Sheriff already held a warrant. The agreement was reported in *Court Business* of May 1979. It was agreed that when a Bailiff, endeavouring to execute a warrant, learns that the Sheriff's Officer is in possession, he should confirm by telephone call to either the Under Sheriff or to the Officer as soon as possible. The Bailiff is instructed to return his warrant to the Court office who will in turn contact the Under Sheriff to establish priority. If it is found that the County Court execution has priority the Bailiff will take responsibility for proceeding with the levy, otherwise he is to levy to protect the interests of the creditor and then arrange for his warrant to be sent to the Under Sheriff for further action.

Attention was drawn to the need to retain copies of all documents and to ensure that receipt of the warrant was acknowledged by the Under Sheriff.

Charges

The Officer is not entitled to seek a fee for the execution of a County Court warrant, although he may recover out of pocket expenses such as removal charges, nor may he delay the execution of such a warrant where a writ of *fi:fa* is being held over while instalments are paid.

Transfer of Judgments

The execution of all judgments obtained where the subject of the debt is default of an agreement regulated by the Consumer Credit Act 1974, must be performed by the County Court, (art.8(1), High Court and County Court Jurisdiction (Amendment) Order 1993, SI 1993 No. 1407).

In the case of other monetary judgments, a judgment obtained in the County Court in excess of £5,000 must be transferred to the High Court for execution as a writ of *fi:fa*, (art.8(1)(a)); and by art.8(1)(c), a County Court judgment for between £2,000 and £5,000 may, if the creditor so wishes, be transferred to the High Court for enforcement as a writ of *fi:fa*. Below £2,000 execution will remain with the County Court.

Effect of Transfer

When such a transfer has been effected, execution will proceed as though the writ followed a High Court judgment; interest is allowed from the date of the certificate of judgment and fees are charged under the Sheriff's scale. Applications to the Court, affecting and during the conduct of the warrant, will be made to the High Court, except for any application to set aside or vary the original judgment which will be heard in the County Court (RSC, O.45/1/38).

There is no power to transfer an order for possession of land from the County Court to the High Court for execution by the Sheriff.

CONCURRENT WRITS

By RSC, O.47, r.2:

"(1) A party entitled to enforce a judgment or order by writ of *fieri facias* may issue two or more such writs, directed to the sheriffs of different counties, at either the same time or different times, to enforce that judgment or order, but no more shall be levied under all those writs together than is authorised to be levied under one of them."

"(2) Where a party issues two or more writs of *fieri facias* directed to the sheriffs of different counties to enforce the same judgment he must inform each sheriff of the issue of the other writ or writs."

A judgment creditor may issue simultaneous writs of *fi:fa* based on one judgment to several Sheriffs, but it is not permissible to issue several writs of *fi:fa* to the same Sheriff for the recovery of one judgment unless a return has been made to the earlier writ (*Foster v. Baker* (1910) 2 KB 636; *Rothschild v. Fisher* (1920) 2 KB 243). A creditor may not issue a series of small executions on a judgment aggregating the whole except where one writ is for the debt and the other for costs taxed at a later date. The concept of the County Court "part writ" does not exist in the High Court jurisdiction.

The issuing party is obliged to inform each Sheriff of any concurrent writ. Officers should keep their colleagues in other counties fully informed as to the conduct of any concurrent writ as it is essential to avoid levying for an excessive amount.

Restriction on Levy

The reference in the rule to "no more shall be levied" is to ensure that the debtor does not suffer as a result of simultaneous executions. The total charges payable by the debtor may not exceed those which would have been incurred on one writ alone. If the execution is wholly satisfied in one county, the other writ must be withdrawn.

CHAPTER 3

The Writ of Fieri Facias

The writ of *fieri facias* is a writ of execution directing a particular Sheriff to seize and sell sufficient of the judgment debtor's goods and chattels found within his bailiwick to satisfy the judgment and the costs of so doing. The term *"fieri facias"* derives from the Latin *"quod fieri facias de bonis"* meaning "which you shall cause to be made of the goods". The writ does not entitle the Sheriff to hold or to use the goods seized, but only entitles him to proceed to sale unless payment is made in full or the writ is withdrawn.

The Address

The writ will show, as an endorsement (which does not form part of the writ), the address at which execution should take place. The direction is often altered by a letter of instruction from the issuing solicitor. It is the duty of the Sheriff to levy upon the debtor's goods wherever they are found within his bailiwick. From this one could assume that the Officer should attend at any address at which he has reason to believe there are goods of the debtor. However, if the Officer attempts to levy at an address he has discovered personally and it is found that the debtor has nothing there, the Sheriff may be liable in an action for trespass.

If the Sheriff is given inaccurate information by the creditor or by his solicitor, the party instructing him may be liable for any trespass (*Morris v. Salberg* (1899) 22 QB 614; *Rowles v. Senior* (1846) 8 QB 677). In practice, the Officer should only attend at the address given and should not attend at an address of his own discovery until instructed to do so by the creditor. To ensure fullest protection for the Officer, such instructions should be in writing. In any event, the location of the address should be checked in advance; the Sheriff may not levy outside his shrievalty. His authority ends at his boundary.

Royal Residences

Royal residences enjoy the privilege of exemption from execution. This does not apply to a residence which has been abandoned or has officially ceased to be a royal residence, for example, Hampton Court Palace (*Attorney General v. Dakin* (1870) 19 WR 1111). The Palace of Westminster does not count as a Royal Residence (*Combe v. De la Bere* (1882) 31 WR 258) but execution cannot be levied within its precincts without disturbing Parliamentary privilege.

Third Parties' Premises

Premises of a third party should not be entered by the Officer without the consent of the occupier even though the Officer believes that goods of the debtor may be within. *Per* Lawrence, J in *Green v. Leney & Another* (1933) (unreported), "The law has been laid down for many years in this way, that if a Sheriff enters the house of another person it is at his peril whether the goods which the Sheriff has authority to seize be found there or not, and if they are not found there he is a trespasser."

DIPLOMATS

Persons having diplomatic immunity as ambassadors or servants to ambassadors enjoy privilege and are protected from execution (Diplomatic Privileges Acts, 1964-1971). There are some 15,000 persons in the UK enjoying this protection.

Duty as to Inquiry

It is not necessary for the plaintiff to inform the Sheriff of any privilege, it is for the Sheriff to make inquiries should there be doubt. The Foreign and Commonwealth Office in London maintain a register of all diplomats and of all diplomatic premises. They should be contacted for information as to status. Their records are maintained under embassy headings, so it is necessary to establish the debtor's country of origin before the inquiry can be made.

Procedure

It does not appear to be necessary for prior inquiry to be made before attendance on the warrant. The debtor, if entitled to immunity, will be at liberty to claim. Once a claim has been made, a search of the records, by telephone if possible, will establish the authenticity or otherwise of the claim. If the Foreign Office confirm immunity, the Sheriff must withdraw immediately and may not pursue the writ further.

On attendance, if circumstances lead the Officer to suspect that he may be proceeding against protected persons or against protected premises, he should act with caution and should not attempt to levy or remove until he has completed his enquiries.

Diplomatic Premises

An Ambassador is entitled to the free enjoyment of the premises he occupies, whether for business or personal purposes, and the contents of those premises may be claimed as being privileged by that Ambassador. This is of importance where a warrant is directed to business premises which may be occupied by a trading concern which is under the control of a foreign government. To all intents and purposes the building will be a normal office but the foreign government may have had the address recorded as being "diplomatic". Again, enquiries must be made at the Foreign Office, who maintain a record of all protected premises.

It is possible for an application for registration as "diplomatic" to be made after the Sheriff's Officer has levied. In such an instance the levy would be lawful and valid but any further attendance to remove would be unlawful. However, the Foreign Office seldom grant immunity without a full investigation as to need and there tends to be a delay in registration.

Foreign Companies

Commercial operations conducted by a foreign government

are not necessarily exempt from execution (*Alcom v. Republic of Colombia*, (1984) 2 All ER 6).

ACCESS

The Right to Enter Forcibly

The early *Semayne's Case* (1604) 77 ER 194, is leading authority on the question of forcible entry to levy.

> "In all cases where the door is open, the Sheriff may enter the house, and do execution, at the suit of any subject, either of the body or of the goods.
> "In all cases when the King is party, the Sheriff, if doors be not open, may break the party's house either to arrest him or to do other execution of the King's process, if otherwise he cannot enter. But before he breaks it, he ought to signify the cause of his coming and make request to open the doors."

But it was resolved that it is not lawful for the Sheriff, on request made and denial, at the suit of a common person, to break into the debtor's house to execute any process at the suit of any subject.

And, in a later matter, it was confirmed that the Sheriff may enter a debtor's house when the door is open but may only force entry if the Crown is a party (*Kerby v. Denby* (1836) 1 M & W 336).

In an action brought by a County Court Bailiff, it was held that a Bailiff had no right to force his way into a debtor's house for the purpose of gaining entry to enforce a warrant of execution. Even if the door is opened peacefully by the debtor, the Bailiff or Officer cannot thereafter use force to prevent the debtor from shutting the door (*Vaughan v. Mackenzie* (1969) 1 QB 557).

The Sheriff may break into a third party's house if goods have been taken there to avoid execution, but he does so at his own risk. There appears to be no distinction between the house of a debtor and a house in which he is residing with the consent of another. Thus, the debtor's house is that in which he usually resides but does not necessarily own (*Johnson v. Leigh* (1815) 6 Taunt 246; *Ratcliffe v. Burton* (1802) 6 B & P 223; *Hutchinson v. Birch* (1812) 4 Taunt 619; *Cooke v. Birt* (1814) 5 Taunt 765).

In all cases, a demand to enter and a refusal are necessary (*White v. Wiltshire* (1619) Pelm 52; *De Gonduin v. Lewis* (1839) 9 LJ QB 148). However, no demand and refusal are necessary for the purpose of breaking inner doors (*Lee v. Gansell* (1774) Cowp 1; *Hutchinson v. Birch* (1812) *supra*; *Johnson v. Leigh* (1815) *supra*).

The Sheriff may, if necessary, break open the outer door of a barn or out-house detached from a dwelling house, without previous demand and refusal of admission, for the purpose of executing a writ of *fi:fa*, (*Penton v. Brown* (1640) 1 Keb 698; *American Concentrated Meat Co. v. Hendry and Another* (1893) WN 67, 82). The rule that the Sheriff may not break open the outer door of a house does not extend to a shop which is used only as a place of business, (*Hodder v. Williams* (1895) 44 WR 98; *Penton v. Brown* (1640) *supra*).

Generally

For the purpose of levying execution, rather than for removing goods after seizure, entry may not be forced to residential premises, nor to business or trade premises where these are physically attached to, and form part of, the residence.

Where the premises are used solely for business purposes, entry may be forced to levy provided that the Officer has a genuine reason to believe that there are goods of the debtor within. It would be prudent to ensure first that the premises are indeed those of the debtor.

As to what constitutes breaking in, the authorities are mixed. It is doubted if lifting a latch on a door amounts to breaking but opening a window which is shut but not fastened is (*Nash v. Lucas* (1867) LR 2 QB 199). But a window that is open may be further opened to allow entry. Climbing over a wall is not breaking in (*Long v. Clarke* (1894) 1 QB 199).

Where execution has already been levied, the Officer may force entry to regain possession of the goods seized (*Pugh v. Griffiths* (1838) 7 Ad & E 827). See also ch.5, WALKING POSSESSION.

THE LEVY

The term "levy" implies the seizure of goods and chattels to enforce payment of the debt and costs under threat of sale. It does not mean "obtain the money" or "remove the goods".

It is not necessary for the goods to be removed for a levy to take place. The Officer makes a formal seizure of the goods on the premises and will normally obtain a walking possession agreement. This agreement is referred to later in greater detail.

It is not necessary for a full and detailed inventory to be taken for the levy to be effective, indeed a levy of part is good for levy of the whole (*Cole v. Davies* (1698) 1 Ld Raym Cases 725).

Practice

The procedure recommended is:

1. Check that the address is indeed that given on the warrant.
2. Inquire as to whether the occupants have a connexion with the debtor.
3. Inquire as to whether the debtor has goods at the premises.
4. Inquire as to whether the debtor has the use of the premises.

Once these questions have been answered satisfactorily, a levy should be made on the goods of the debtor or on other goods apparently in the order and disposition of the debtor, subject to any third party claims that may be made.

We suggest that the essential part of the levy is to ensure that the debtor is made aware of the execution and of the actual taking of the goods into the custody of the Sheriff. There is little point in attending, handing over some forms and then leaving the premises. The true nature of the warrant ought to be explained to a responsible person. The personal presence of the debtor is not necessary.

Although not a legal requirement as in rent or tax distress, written notice of the execution should be left at the premises. The detail in the notice should include a statement that the goods have been taken into the custody of the Sheriff and that they may not be disposed of, or dealt with, without the permission of the Sheriff. It is advisable for the notice to include a requirement for third parties to make any claim to ownership in writing. Ideally, the notice should also incorporate a statement of the amount due and indicate that interest (if any) and Sheriff's charges are accruing. See *post,* ch.5 for a suggested form of notice.

Care must be taken in matters where the value of the goods may not warrant the costs of removal and sale; where the premises are occupied by several inter-related companies; residential premises where the debtor may have vacated the matrimonial home or where the debtor lodges as a member of the family; third party's premises such as bonded warehouses and those where it is apparent that the debtor has no effects. These matters, and others, are dealt with below.

Goods of Low Value

The lack of realizable assets does not prevent a debtor from satisfying an execution but the Officer should not expect to recover possession money if he has not levied on items he is able to sell. It is advisable to leave the notice of the execution as though a levy were being made; then to indicate to the solicitors for the creditor that this has been done in spite of the lack of value, in the hope that payment or a reasonable offer of payment may be made. If no success is achieved within a week or so, the warrant should be withdrawn to enable the creditor to proceed by alternative means. The fee the Officer may expect to recover from the creditor should not exceed that which would have been charged if the warrant had been returned abortive in the first instance.

Inter-Related Companies

It is not uncommon for a group of companies to occupy

the same premises. However, the Officer must bear in mind that a body corporate must be dealt with in the same way as an individual debtor and the interests of the other members of the group are entitled to be protected. A levy should be made and each member of the group invited to submit a claim to ownership of their effects.

Families

The Officer must set himself apart from the personal problems of the debtor or the debtor's family. The warrant is directed to the goods and chattels of the debtor, not against his person. If the household effects belong to the debtor, albeit absent, a levy should be made. It is not unusual for an estranged partner to claim an interest in the furniture and domestic equipment. In such an instance he or she should be invited to submit a claim to ownership of part or joint interest. If necessary, the Court can adjudicate on the claim and make an order as to sale and division of the proceeds of such a sale.

Member of a Family

Many executions are directed to premises which prove to be those of the debtor's parents, the debtor merely residing there as a member of the family or as a lodger. In such instance, a levy may be made and the parents and indeed any other relatives should be invited to make such claims to ownership as need be. It is not uncommon for such a debtor to possess at least some effects and provided these are not exempt from execution they should be seized. A simple example of this situation is the grant of credit to a teenager to buy a motor bicycle or hi-fi unit.

The creditor may be asked to indicate the basis of the judgment debt if it is considered that that may aid identification of assets available for seizure.

Third Party Premises

Executions are frequently directed to warehouses, or indeed to any other premises not owned and occupied by the debtor, but where the debtor may have effects stored.

The Officer may only enter the premises with the consent of the occupant and may only levy on the debtor's effects subject to any lien the occupant may have. Whilst it is possible to interplead on a lien, caution should be exercised lest accruing storage charges be invoiced to the Officer.

A levy should be made, confined to the goods of the debtor, as identified by the occupant; details of any lien requested; instructions requested from the creditor's solicitors and the matter dealt with expeditiously to avoid unnecessary cost or damages arising. It is not permissible to add the lien to the judgment and for the sale to proceed to satisfy both. That can only be done after an application to the Court and an appropriate Order has been made.

Companies in Private Residences

With the increase in the formation of small limited liability companies, many executions direct the Sheriff to seize the effects of a company at a private house, usually that of a director.

An attendance must be made, and a levy if there are goods of the company to be found there. A claim is required to the rest of the contents. However, the goods may consist of little more than documents if the address be used solely for receiving mail. There is little point in making a levy if the Officer is satisfied that the premises are purely residential. Nevertheless it does no harm to seek a letter of confirmation from the occupant and certainly it is a good idea to ask for the location of a trading address.

By s.348(1) of the Companies Act 1985, a company must display its name outside every address from which it conducts business. However, the absence of such a name plate does not necessarily imply there are no effects within.

Registered Offices

There is nothing to be gained in levying an execution at premises that are used only as the debtor company's registered office, which may be only occupied by accountants or solicitors. If possible, a trading address should be obtained which may be reported to the creditor for further instructions.

Third Party Claims - General

Where any person merely suggests to an Officer that the debtor has no effects at the premises, the Officer must decide for himself whether or not to levy. The best course, if in doubt, is to ask there and then for a written notice of claim to the goods on the premises. If such a claim is not forthcoming, or is suspect in any way, the Officer should levy and seek instructions under the Order 17 procedure when a claim is finally submitted. The Officer is obliged to make reasonable enquiries before proceeding to a removal and sale. The definition of "reasonable" will vary according to the circumstances and according to the status of the persons who have knowledge of the execution (see *Observer v. Gordon* (1983) 1 WLR 1008 and ch.6, CLAIMS).

Instructions Contrary to Public Policy

The Sheriff cannot be forced to deal with goods contrary to public policy. For example, he cannot be instructed to seize and sell pornographic materials. Likewise, we doubt if he can be instructed to obtain entry to premises or possession of goods by means of trickery. If the Officer is in doubt, the Sheriff may apply to the Court for directions.

Harassment

Officers executing a warrant are not considered to be harassing debtors. Section 40 of the Administration of Justice Act 1970 states:

1(a) ... "does not apply to anything done by a person which is reasonable (and otherwise permissible in Law) for the purpose -
(b) of the enforcement of any liability by legal process."

CHAPTER 4

Goods & Chattels
Seizable Under a Fi:Fa

By s.138(3A), Supreme Court Act 1981 (added by s.15, Courts and Legal Services Act 1990), the Sheriff may seize all, or as much as may be necessary, of the available goods and chattels of the judgment debtor. The subsection reads:

"Every sheriff or officer executing any writ of execution issuing from the High Court against the goods of any person may by virtue of it seize -

(a)   any of that person's goods except

    (i)   Such tools, books, vehicles and other items of equipment as are necessary to that person for use personally by him in his employment, business or vocation;

    (ii)   Such clothing, bedding, furniture and other items of equipment as are necessary for satisfying the basic domestic needs of that person and his family; and

(b)   any money, banknotes, bills of exchange, promissory notes, bonds, specialities or security for money belonging to that person."

Per Mr Piers Ashworth, QC sitting as a Deputy Judge in *John Kenneth Moffat v. Lemkin (formerly High Sheriff of Greater London)* (1993) (unreported):

> "Although the wording has changed from previous Acts of Parliament, the limits on the sheriff's powers of seizure are still expressed in a similar way to earlier acts: *prima facie* the sheriff has a right, indeed a duty to seize all the goods of the judgment debtor."

By s.(4)(c), *ibid.*, any reference to "the goods" includes anything else that may be lawfully seized in execution.

The term "chattels" is one of the widest known to the law in terms of personal property and it appears that it may include for instance, shares in a company (*Robinson v. Jenkins* (1890) 24 QBD 275) or title deeds to property (*Roberts v. Bell* (1857) 7 E & B 323). However, it may be that to reach certain classes of chattels, the creditor must apply for the appointment of a Receiver.

It should be noted that there is no monetary restriction specified in the exemption sub-clauses in the Act, no value above which the exemptions do not apply.

In *Toseland Building Supplies v. Bishop* (Court of Appeal (October 28, 1993) unreported), Steyn, LJ held that the amendment to the law does not preclude the Sheriff from seizing all the goods in the first place notwithstanding that some may later be held to be "tools of trade", and the burden rests firmly with the judgment debtor to raise the issue that some or all of the goods so seized may be "tools of trade". Steyn, LJ said "...it must be said that when the Sheriff seizes goods, he seizes all the goods, and if the judgment debtor maintains that some are tools of trade then the burden is on him to raise this as an issue". See also for example *Gonsky v. Durrell* (1918) 2 KBR 71.

And in *Moffatt, supra,* the Deputy Judge held that it was for the debtor to establish that goods fall within the exemptions. In both of these cases it was decided that the claimed tools of trade must be for the exclusive personal use of the debtor. It follows from this that a corporate entity cannot claim an exemption for tools of trade.

It appears also that a claim made by the debtor and disputed by the creditor can be brought before the court for decision as the subject of interpleader proceedings (*Toseland Building Supplies Ltd v. Bishop* (1993) *supra*). Again *per* Steyn, LJ "there is a clear issue to be decided and it matters not how this issue finds its way to this Court but this Court will decide it."

In the *Moffat* case, the Deputy Judge voiced a word of caution, "It is submitted to me that there must be a duty upon the Sheriff to advise a debtor whose goods are being seized of the provisions of s.138 and the procedure to be adopted ... it is said it would be monstrous if that were not the law."

"I do not accept that there is any such duty upon the Sheriff to the claimant, although I do accept that it would, certainly to a layman, be monstrous for a sheriff to sell goods which were likely tools of trade without any warning."

It is suggested practice therefore, to quote the advice of the Under Sheriff of Surrey, "that when Officers come across goods which in their view do clearly fall within the exemption clauses then it will be prudent to raise with the debtor immediately whether he wishes to raise a claim under the exemptions or not. Most debtors will be in complete ignorance of the law on this matter and it is better that claims under the exemptions are dealt with at the outset of an execution than after goods have been sold."

The Sheriff may only seize goods which he can sell and

there are particular restrictions on seizure of certain
other assets such as debts, equitable interest in
leaseholds and, to some extent, farming stock and crops.
Generally, certain categories of goods require particular
attention and there are many categories of goods which
have attracted statutory regulation which must be
observed by the Sheriff. The following notes may assist
and see also the notes in ch.9, SALE OF GOODS.

Aeroplanes

Execution may be issued against airlines and against
foreign governments who operate airlines on a commercial
basis and a warrant may direct the Officer to seize a
particular aircraft.

Aircraft are documented in a manner similar to ships.
They are registered in a specific country and a register
is maintained in that country, which shows the details
of the aircraft, details of any charges registered and the
identity of the owner. Most aircraft engaged in
international flights are obliged to display a plate,
showing the registration number of the aeroplane and the
identity of the owner, in a manner which allows it to be
seen by persons entering.

In the cockpit should be found documents appertaining
to the aircraft such as an insurance certificate, details of
registration, details relating to the servicing and the
airworthiness certificate. There is a requirement to leave
the registration certificate on board, similar to that
specified in s.15, Merchant Shipping Act, 1894.

Commercial aircraft operators must comply with
stringent safety requirements and full maintenance
records are kept for each individual part of the aircraft.
These records will be retained at the place of normal

servicing. If the sale of the aircraft is to take place, access to these records is essential. Without them, any buyer must assume that all parts have a zero life and must be renewed. The aircraft in these circumstances would have only scrap value.

Seizure of the aircraft is effected by affixing a copy of the warrant to both the inside (in the cockpit) and to the outside. The interior copy is to advise any pilot that he flies the aircraft at his peril and the exterior copy to advise any persons entering the aircraft that it is the subject of a seizure. The airport authorities should be asked to ensure that no flight plan is accepted and airport security should be advised of the seizure. To immobilize the aeroplane, chocks such as heavy concrete blocks can be placed by the wheels. It is not advisable to interfere with the mechanics of the plane in any way.

The insurers of the aircraft should be informed of the seizure and asked to note the interest of the Sheriff. They should be asked to advise the Sheriff if any steps are taken to alter or cancel the insurance cover. In the absence of adequate insurance, application should be made to the court for an Order. In the case of *Twist v. East African Airways Corporation* (1977) (unreported), a party to the interpleader was ordered to insure the Boeing 707 against third party claims, fire and for taxiing only.

If the aircraft is the subject of a charge or mortgage, the Officer should make the customary enquiries, seek a proper claim and submit this to the creditor's solicitors. Elements of the aircraft may belong to different parties. The engines may not be in the same ownership as the airframe; the electronic navigation systems may belong to a completely different company and so on.

When dealing with commercial aircraft, speed of action is of the essence as costs will mount with alacrity. If any error is made, damages can be high and subsequent litigation could be of an international nature.

Animals

Animals and livestock are available for seizure but the Officer must ensure that they are cared for and properly fed. The cost of feeding, if met by the Officer and not by the owner, may be added to the Sheriff's charges.

An animal seized may not be worked but cows should be milked when necessary. The Ministry of Agriculture, Fisheries & Food (MAFF) has power to control the movement of animals, particularly when moved to and from auction sales. If there are local regulations in force (for example, those enforced when there is an outbreak of foot and mouth disease or swine vasicular fever in the district), the Officer is obliged to comply with such regulations.

There are regulations controlling the sale of animals in markets, principally The Welfare of Horses at Markets (and Other Places of Sale) Order 1990, (SI 1990 No.2627) and The Welfare of Animals at Markets Order 1990 (SI 1990 No.2628). The first order created the offences of "permitting an unfit horse to be exposed for sale in a market" (art.5(1)), "permitting a mare to be exposed for sale in a market if it is likely to give birth while it is there", (art.5(2)), "bringing a foal to market unless it is at the foot of its dam," (art.7(1)), "exposing for sale a foal separately from its dam," (art.7(2)), "separating a foal from its dam while in a market" (art.7(3)).

The order does not prohibit the seizure and sale of horses, nor mares in foal or with foals at foot. The second order repeats the provisions of the first so far as pregnant or unfit animals are concerned and creates similar offences. In the second order, the definition of animals includes cattle, sheep, goats and all other ruminants, pigs, rabbits and poultry. A market includes a market place or sale yard and any other premises to which animals are brought and exposed for sale, together with any lairage and parking place used by visitors to the sale.

There are also new (1993) regulations concerning documentation of male cattle. It is presently illegal to own male cattle over three months old without being in possession of a Cattle Identification Document (CID) and if sold, the seller must be in possession of the CID. Inspectors appointed by MAFF can demand production of these documents at any time. If such animals are seized, ear tags should be carefully checked against CID's to ensure proper identification.

We are advised that where the execution debtor refuses to surrender CIDs to facilitate sale, the Sheriff could apply to the Regional Service Centre of MAFF for new documents in the name of the Sheriff to allow the cattle to be sold. Alternatively, it is conceived that the Sheriff could apply to the court for directions under RSC, O.15, r.16. (See also HORSES).

Caravans

A caravan may be seized provided it has not become a fixture. A caravan which may be towed may be seized but a caravan standing on brick pillars may not. The attachment of services such as electricity is not a true test. Certain caravans may be used for .permanent residence, technically becoming "real estate" rather than "goods and chattels". It would be open to the debtor and occupier to apply to the court to seek exemption from seizure.

No caravan should be removed while occupied as the

Officer may be charged with abduction (*Cave v. Capel* (1954) 1 QB 367). We doubt if the Officer has the right to evict an occupant to facilitate the sale of a caravan under an execution without further order of the court.

Computers

In seizing such equipment it must be remembered that the sale price will be minimal unless all the necessary operating systems, instruction books, interface cables etc, are also seized and unless they are current models still maintained by the manufacturer.

Certain operating systems, particularly those relating to the larger and more complex computers, and much application software, are usually subject to a "Licence to Use". This may not be transferable on sale, and will reflect in the saleability of the system.

While the actual machine and supporting documents may be seized, it is unlikely that a writ of *fi:fa* extends to the information contained in a data base. If removal were to take place, it would be prudent to leave the discs or tapes which do not relate to the operating system. The debtor can be invited to back up information held on the hard drive memory of the machine to tape or disc, if he so wishes, subsequently deleting data he considers to be confidential to him.

Documents and Business Records

Where these have no intrinsic value, they are not available for seizure. However, in the judgment of Glidewell, J in *Observer v. Gordon* (1983) 1 WLR 1008, it was said that the Sheriff was permitted to examine the available records of a debtor if such action was necessary to establish ownership of assets seized, but in that case the debtor had died after the levy, leaving no personal representative or executor willing to take responsibility for the estate.

It has been known for a creditor to instruct the Sheriff to seize and offer for sale such records as address lists, patterns etc. Before agreeing to such a request, the Officer should make full enquiries as to copyright ownership. The court has made orders authorizing the sale of master tapes and videos provided that they be offered with a specific warning that copyright does not pass to the purchaser.

Executors and Administrators

Goods held on behalf of the estate of a deceased person may not be taken in execution issued personally against the executor or administrator (*Farr v. Newman* (1792) 4 TR 621); *Foley v. Burnell* (1783) 1 BCC 278). However, if they have used the goods as if they were their own, the goods will not be exempt (*Quick v. Staines* (1798) 2 Esp 657; *Ray v. Ray* (1815) Coop 264; *Fenwick v. Laycock* (1841) 2 QB 108).

A *fi:fa* issued against the estate of a deceased person should direct the Sheriff to the goods held by the executor on behalf of the estate. It should not extend to the executor's personal assets, but may authorize seizure of the executor's goods for costs if no goods remain of the estate. A *fi:fa* issued prior to the death of the debtor is good against the estate of that debtor. The death must be after the teste date of the writ (*Thoroughgood's Case*, (1598) Noy 73).

Death of an execution creditor does not affect the

operation of the writ; the Sheriff will account to the deceased creditor's estate or personal representative.

Farms

By the Agricultural Credits Act, 1928, a charge may be placed on the assets of a farm and that charge will be good against an execution creditor even while uncrystallized. It is open to the creditor to dispute the claim despite lack of an appointed receiver. A register is maintained at the Land Registry of all charges under the Act, and the execution creditor should be asked for a copy of the search in all matters where the address for levy is a farm or where the Sheriff believes that the debtor is a farmer as defined in s.5 of the Act.

The procedure to be followed is for the Officer to seize but not to proceed to a sale until it has been established that there is no prior charge. Should the search prove positive, the holder of the charge must be approached and invited to lodge with the Sheriff a notice to the effect that the execution must not proceed until the charge is satisfied. It should be stressed that the above applies only to charges registered under the Act, and not necessarily to any loan made to a farmer.

Farming stock and crops are available for execution, but are subject to some restrictions. There is a distinction between crops which mature within a year, and those (as with some fruit) which take longer. See *Mather*, 3rd edn, pp.318/323.

Firearms

Control of firearms is vested in the Police Authority and

is subject to the Firearms Act 1968, the Firearms (Amendment) Act 1988 and the Firearms Acts (Amendment) Regulations 1992. The principal act, as amended, divides firearms into three main categories:

1. Prohibited weapons as defined in s.5 of the 1968 Act together with certain other weapons considered especially dangerous.
2. Weapons that can only be held on a firearms certificate issued in accordance with s.1. of the principal act.
3. Shotguns, which must be covered by certificate under s.2.

A shotgun is defined as being a smooth-bore gun (not being an air weapon) of an overall length of greater than 40 inches having a barrel not less than 24 inches long, and a bore of not more than two inches diameter. Further, the gun may not have a magazine capable of holding more than two rounds and may not be a revolver gun.

Prohibited weapons comprise machine guns, self loading or pump action rifles other than .22 rim-fire guns, shotguns outside the dimensions stated above; for example, sawn-offs, smooth-bore revolvers other than those chambered for 9mm rim-fire cartridges or muzzle loaded, rocket launchers, mortars except those designed for line throwing or pyrotechnic purposes. Also prohibited are firearms disguised as something else, (for example, a walking stick), explosive rockets for military use and in general most military weapons.

Prohibited weapons may only be possessed, sold or transferred if the holder is granted a specific licence which is not usually granted to private individuals but may be granted to *bona fide* collectors or museums.

Section 1 firearms comprise, by default, all other

legally held guns which are not either shotguns as defined above or prohibited weapons.

Antiques for static display purposes only are generally outside the requirements for certification but should carry a certificate of de-activation issued by a proof house.

The restrictions on s.1 firearms are quite stringent. The police must be approached for any variation of the certificate, which is specific to the weapons held, before any transfer or purchase can be legally undertaken. There are however no restrictions on the holding, purchase or sale of additional s.2 shotguns provided that the police are satisfied that the scale of such operations does not amount to dealing for which a dealer's certificate is required. Ammunition for firearms may only be acquired on production of the relevant certificate; in the case of s.1 guns, the quantity that may be held or purchased will be specified in the certificate.

Sales may be made to visiting persons from EC and other states but, unless the gun is entirely within the bounds covered by a shotgun certificate and the buyer holds a visitor's shotgun permit, the buyer must produce a licence issued by the Department of Trade and Industry for its export unless he can show that the gun will be exported directly to a non-EC state or unless he can show that he is purchasing the gun for a licensed collector or museum and the gun is acquired exclusively for the purposes of display in an historical or cultural collection.

Firearms may not be pawned (s.3(6) 1968 Act), nor may a shotgun or ammunition be given to a person under the age of 15 years (s.24(3) *ibid*).

Firearms may not be carried loaded and should always be covered by a case or suitable slip in a public place.

For the purposes of the Sheriff, firearms may be transported by an auctioneer, carrier or warehouseman without the necessity of a certificate (s.9(1), 1968 Act) but it is an offence to fail to take reasonable precautions for the gun's safe custody, or to fail to report to the police the loss or theft of it, (s.14, 1988 Act). The same applies to ammunition.

An auctioneer is not required to hold a dealer's certificate but must obtain a permit to sell firearms from the police, (s.9(2), 1968 Act).

Firearms and ammunition may in general only be sold to persons who have a certificate authorizing their possession or to a person acting on behalf of a museum which holds a museum firearms licence. The seller and buyer must each inform the police of the transaction within seven days.

By the Gun Barrel Proof Act it is illegal to sell by auction a gun that is out of proof even if it is advertised and labelled as such. Such a firearm may be sold as separate components, eg, stock, action and barrels, but to different buyers.

The prudent Officer, seizing guns or ammunition of any description, will liaise with the local police on doing so to ensure that he remains within the scope of the acts and does not commit by mistake one of the numerous offences in this connexion.

Fixtures

Only assets of a debtor may be seized, assets which the debtor is at liberty to sell. Fixtures which have become landlord's fixtures may not be sold (*Pooles Case* (1703) 1 Selk 368).

Whether the asset is a fitting or a fixture is a question of fact but, as a rule of thumb, any asset which when removed would damage the fabric of the building is most likely to have become the landlord's. For example, an item attached to the wall with a screw is capable of removal without damage to the building but the same may not apply when affixed by nails or adhesive substance.

Where the debtor is the freeholder, only "trade fixtures" may be seized. These are fixtures which have not become part of the freehold, for example, ranges and ovens would be passed with the sale of the freehold thus placing them outside the scope of the writ (*Winn v. Ingilby* (1822) 5 B & Ald 625).

A further example of the distinction between fixtures and fittings is that of seating in a place of entertainment. Were the seats individual in structure and affixed to the floor purely to comply with Local Authority regulations they would be fittings (*Lyon & Co v. London City & Midland Bank* (1903) 88 LT 392). Had the seats been manufactured in blocks of, say, four and attached to the floor by means of iron standards they would be deemed to be fixtures (*Vaudeville Electric Cinema Ltd v. Muriset* (1923) 129 LT 446 and see *Mather*, 3rd edn, p.324 *et seq*).

Furnished Tenancies

The Sheriff may not interfere with the free enjoyment of a third party in assets of the debtor. Therefore furniture which is let, hired or rented to another cannot be seized, (*Rumball v. Murray* 3 T & R 298; *Miller v. Farnell* 2 Marsh 78; 6 Taunt).

Goods in Bond or Awaiting Import

Provided the goods are within the bailiwick of the Sheriff to whom the writ is directed they are available for seizure. However, any sale which results in the effects being removed may only take place provided all taxes due are secured. Prior and close liaison with the local tax authorities will be essential. The authority for seizure and sale lies within the command of the writ.

Goods Sold by the Debtor

Although the goods of a debtor are bound in his hands from the time of lodgment of the writ, this does not extend to items sold for valuable consideration and in good faith, provided the purchaser did not have knowledge of the writ, (s.138(2), Supreme Court Act 1981).

Any debtor who has execution levied against his assets is entitled to indicate those items which are already sold but awaiting delivery and the Officer is obliged to disregard such items if the debtor's allegation is substantiated.

Hosiery Machines

Hosiery making frames, looms etc which are being worked are exempt from seizure and from distress by the landlord, unless execution or distress is issued against the actual owner of the machine. This is to permit an "outdoor worker" to have such machines, perhaps the property of his employer, on his premises but to ensure they are not seized under a warrant issued against that outdoor worker, (s.18, Hosiery Act, 1843 as amended 1968).

Horses

Horses may be classified in three categories: those used as pets for informal riding; those used for sporting events (excluding racing); those used for racing.

The first category may be regarded as "general animals" and dealt with accordingly. The remaining categories consist of horses which are registered with a society. Thoroughbreds are generally recorded at Wetherbys but other horses may be registered with a society by virtue of their breeding or by virtue of the competitions in which they are entered. Irish horses are registered with the Irish Horse Board in Dublin. The important point to note is that these animals have registration documents identifying the animal and its ownership. To achieve the best price at sale, possession of the documents is required. Additional identifying papers will include the vaccination record which may be held by the vet or by the person caring for the animal.

Insurance Policies

As the Sheriff may not sign on behalf of a debtor, the Officer cannot be in a position to surrender a policy. The appropriate procedure would be for the execution creditor to proceed by means of Equitable Execution and seek the appointment of a receiver.

It appears the only "investments" available for seizure are bearer bonds or similar items which can be transferred by simple delivery rather than by signature.

Joint Property

Provided that the debtor has an interest in the property,

the Officer should seize and seek a notice of claim to part from the other persons having an interest. It is open to the court to make an Order for sale and, if appropriate, for the allocation of the proceeds.

It would not be unreasonable for any such Order to require that the Sheriff first invite the claimant to purchase the share of the debtor, a not uncommon event in matters where a husband and wife have a joint interest.

Leases

A debtor's chattel interest in a lease may be seized and sold and possession of the actual lease is not essential. The Sheriff's assignment of the term is sufficient without an actual seizure of the lease (*Coleman v. Rawlinson* (1858) 1 F & F 330). Seizure of the lease does not vest the term in the Sheriff until he has executed an assignment of it and if he remains in possession of the premises he is a trespasser at the suit of the debtor. If this action is taken, it is necessary to register the writ under the Land Charges Act, 1972 or for a caution to be entered in the Land Registry.

However, the sale of the debtor's interest in a lease does not put the purchaser into possession of the property itself; the purchaser must necessarily apply to the Court for a possession order, or, if there is a sub-tenant, may distrain for the rent. (See *Mather*, 3rd edn, pp.106 and 107).

Liens

A lien is a personal right and cannot be seized under a

writ of *fi:fa* (*Legg v. Evans* (1840) 9 LJ(NS) 102; *Rogers v. Kennay* (1846) 9 QB 592).

A person who holds a lien loses the right of lien if he causes execution to be levied as that is parting with possession (*Jacobs v. Latour and Messer* (1828) 5 Bing 129).

Medicines

The sale of medicines is subject to the Medicines Act, 1968 which is enforced by the Pharmaceutical Society of Great Britain.

Under this Act there are four main categories of medicines being:

1.   General sales list medicines.
2.   Pharmacy medicines.
3.   Prescription only medicines, and
4.   Animal medicines which may only be sold by pharmacists or certain authorized agricultural merchants.

Categories 2, 3 and 4 may only be sold by retail from registered pharmacies and the sale must be supervised by a registered pharmaceutical chemist.

All four categories may be sold by wholesale dealing provided that the purchaser is authorized to sell on. In practice this means that categories 2, 3 and 4 can only be sold to registered pharmaceutical chemists or to a doctor, dentist, veterinary surgeon or to persons lawfully conducting a retail pharmacy business, ie, the owner of a pharmacy, or to another wholesaler.

Any person engaged in selling medicines wholesale must possess a wholesale dealers' licence issued by the

Department of Social Security. To proceed to sale without such a licence will leave the Officer liable to prosecution.

These restrictions apply only to sale, not to seizure. The Officer will have an opportunity of clarifying the position before proceeding.

Money, Bank Notes and Cheques

By s.138 (3A), Supreme Court Act 1981 (as amended 1990) "Every sheriff or officer executing any writ of execution issued from the High Court against the goods of any person may by virtue of it seize -

(b) any money, banknotes, bills of exchange, promissory notes, bonds, specialities or securities for money belonging to that person."

This section follows the original provisions of s.12, Judgments Act 1838 with one exception, the deletion of cheques from the list in s.(b). A cheque is of course a form of bill of exchange but the Cheques Act 1992 restricted dealings in such documents. Cheques that are crossed and endorsed 'a/c payee' should only be presented for payment by the payee.

The provisions of the Cheques Act 1992 materially altered the attitude of banks to the presentation of cheques by the Sheriff. Banks will require an indemnity from the Officer or account holder before they will process cheques seized or given to the Sheriff which are not made payable to him. The Officer should exercise the utmost caution when presenting such cheques as he will be liable under his indemnity to the bank or to the drawer in the event of any mistake.

It was further stated in the old act that the Sheriff may hold bonds, promissory notes etc, and may sue in the name of the Sheriff for the recovery of those monies promised, provided that the execution creditor indemnifies the Sheriff against all costs and expenses incurred. There is no reason to believe that the courses of action available to the Sheriff have been altered by the new act. The Sheriff may not sell such documentary credits, he can only recover the proceeds himself. The effect of this section is to make money, bank notes and so on liable to seizure in the same way as other goods and chattels but they do not on seizure vest in the execution creditor.

Money in Court

Section 138(3A) Supreme Court Act 1981 authorizes by analogy the attachment of money in Court (see also *Brereton v. Edwards* (1888) 21 QBD 226).

Monies held by the Sheriff

A balance of monies held after satisfying a prior execution constitutes a debt from the Sheriff to the execution debtor and as a mere debt cannot be taken in execution under a later writ issued after the completion of the prior (*Harrison v. Paynter* (1840) 9 LJ 169; *O'Neill v. Cunningham* (1872) 6 Ir CL 503).

Monies held by a Third Party

Monies in the hand of a third party, acting as trustee for the debtor, cannot be seized (*France v. Campbell* (1842) 9 Dowl 914; *Brown v. Perrot* (1841) 8 Bead 985).

Motor Vehicles

A motor vehicle may be seized and may be sold even though the registration documents are not available.

It is open to question if it is possible to enter into walking possession of a motor vehicle unless it is on enclosed premises or has been immobilized. Until it is necessary to proceed to removal and sale, the Officer should advise the debtor of the existence of the warrant and certainly make it known that the car has been noted. If a claim is received and the vehicle is not in close possession, the claim should be submitted on the basis of "goods about to be seized".

It would be prudent to enquire as to the identity of the registered keeper (at the Driver and Vehicle Licensing Agency at Swansea) and as to the possibility of hire purchase agreement covering the vehicle (at Hire Purchase Information Ltd). HPI also maintain a record of cars that have been the subject of rebuilds after insurance company "write-offs" and it is wise to make enquiries in that respect before a vehicle is sold. (See RSC, O.45/1/18).

It should be remembered that DVLA only retains details of the registered keeper, their records do not show absolute ownership and HPI do not record all hire purchase agreements, only those registered by companies who participate in the scheme. HPI make no distinction between hire purchase and credit sale agreements. However, by making these inquiries, the Officer may be directed to such parties as may have an interest in a vehicle. DVLA inquiries are free of charge but HPI make a charge for a search.

If the vehicle is sold without registration documents, the Officer or the auctioneer should notify, in writing, DVLA of the details of the sale, date and purchaser. This will enable the purchaser to obtain a replacement document.

If the vehicle is a foreign import or is a UK manufactured vehicle on which no car tax or duty has been paid, the local office of the Customs and Excise must be advised. They are entitled to assess the value of the vehicle and seek payment of the tax due. It is usual for them to accept the sale realization as being the value and for the tax to be added to the bid price.

Vehicles imported into the UK upon which no tax has been paid are frequently allocated special registration numbers. Details of these numbers can be obtained from the Customs and Excise.

Imported vehicles may not comply with UK requirements as to roadworthiness. Any sale catalogue should have a note to that effect.

Partnerships

It is essential that Partnerships are not confused with Limited Companies. A partnership does not exist in its own right, it consists of individual people who are trading together. The members are responsible for the debts of the partnership. A limited company has its own legal existence, the members are responsible for the debts only up to the extent of the capital, hence the term "limited liability".

A writ of *fi:fa* may be directed against the assets of a partnership provided that judgment has been obtained against the firm, (s.23, Partnership Act 1890 & RSC, O.81, r.10, and see also the note at O.17/1/12 in *Supreme Court Practice*). However, if it is wished to proceed against the personal assets of an individual partner, his or her name must be incorporated in the command portion of the writ.

The creditor may elect to proceed against either the firm or the individuals or both. The Officer must ensure that execution is levied against only those parties actually identified. It is not uncommon to find a writ of *fi:fa* directed to the private residence of a partner whilst the actual writ is in the name of the firm. Under these circumstances it might be advisable to invite the creditor to apply to have the judgment amended to include the individual. In the absence of such an amendment the individual would be entitled to submit a claim to the effects and an interpleader could ensue.

Where the *fi:fa* is directed solely against an individual partner and the Officer is directed to the partnership assets, the remaining partners are entitled to claim ownership of, or claim an interest in, the assets seized. The correct procedure is for that claim to be submitted under RSC, O.17, r.2 and, if necessary, interpleader proceedings issued (*Peake v. Carter* (1916) 1 KB 652). The Court may elect to make an Order allowing the sale with the proviso that the claimant(s) be paid a proportion. As with joint matrimonial property, it may be wise to seek leave to sell by private treaty, thus allowing the claimant the opportunity of acquiring the assets by purchasing the debtor's interest.

Patient in the Control of the Court of Protection

The goods of a patient are exempt from seizure when in the hands of a Receiver appointed by the Court, but may be sold under the execution if the Receiver is appointed after seizure but before sale (*Re Winkle* (1894) 2 CH 519; *Re Clarke* (1898) 1 CH 336; s.96 Mental Health Act, 1983; RSC, O.45, r.1/22).

Pawnbroker's Interest

A pawnbroker's interest in redeemable pledges may be taken under a *fi:fa (Rollason; Rollason v. Rollason; Halse's Claim* (1887) 35 WR 607).

Pawned Goods

The Sheriff may not seize goods which a debtor has lodged with a third party as security for a debt (*Rogers v. Kenway* (1846) 9 QB 592).

Pawn Tickets

These represent the pawner's equity of redemption which is not seizable under a *fi:fa*. It appears the Sheriff cannot sell pawn tickets but could, if the pawned property lay within his bailiwick, offer the pawnbroker the amount due, redeem the goods and proceed to sale.

Perishable Items

A writ of *fi:fa* is a writ of immediate execution; the Officer should seize and, if not paid, should sell without undue delay lest the goods deteriorate.

All sales by the Sheriff should be in accordance with s.138A (1), Supreme Court Act 1981 which is identical in terms and effect to s.97(1), County Court Act 1984. A sale not conducted in accord with the strict rule is irregular but is valid until set aside (see *Cranshaw v. Harrison* (1894) 1 QB 79 and see also *County Court Practice 1994* at p.85.). By s.93, County Court Act, 1984 there is an exclusion for perishable goods in the requirement to delay sale for five days after the day of seizure, but that section applies only to County Court warrants. In the High Court procedure there is no restriction on the date of sale. Therefore, we submit that in the absence of other authority, the common and age old practice of immediate sale of perishables without advertising and by private contract, may be at best irregular in terms of the statutory requirements.

If the goods be sold in this way, the Officer must ensure that a proper price is obtained.

Police Custody

Items held by the police after an investigation or whilst the debtor is serving a prison sentence may be seized. Such effects fall into the same category as items held by third parties. The Officer may seize only with the permission of the police but it would be unusual for that permission to be withheld unless the effects were required for evidence. The police have their own procedures for dealing with prisoners' assets; they may elect to apply to a magistrate for permission to release the effects to the Officer.

If the effects are required for evidence, say, where there is an allegation of fraud, it may be advisable to reach some practical agreement; for example, for the police to retain samples of the goods, the Officer removing the residue after a full and detailed inventory (possibly including photographs) has been taken.

Railway Rolling Stock

Under s.4, Railway Companies Act, 1867, rolling stock and plant were exempted from any execution commenced after the implementation of the Act. The creditor cannot proceed by means of *fi:fa* but may seek the appointment of a receiver. (See also Transport Acts, 1947 and 1962, and London Regional Transport Act, 1984).

Ships

Seizure is effected by going aboard and affixing a copy of the warrant to the mast. Historically, this was to inform the crew that the vessel was the subject of a seizure. Nowadays, it is sensible to attach a further copy of the warrant to the bridge, putting the master or pilot on notice that they sail at their peril.

Registered ships have their official number carved into the main beam of the ship. On commercial vessels this number is normally to be found on the aft side of the forward beam of the main hatch. A note of the registered tonnage will be found in the same place. The port of registry is not shown there, for this the Officer must look at the stern of the ship (see Merchant Shipping Act, 1894, s.7 as amended).

Fishing vessels are not obliged to show the port of registry on the stern, it is sufficient to be lettered and numbered in accordance with Part 4 of the above act.

The vessel must carry its Certificate of Registry at all times and this document must not be removed. Section 15, Merchant Shipping Act, 1894 requires that this shall be used only for the lawful navigation of the ship and shall not be subject to detention.

The property in a registered vessel is divided into 64 shares, the ownership of these shares is recorded at the Custom House at the port of registry and the Officer may establish the ownership by simple inquiry.

The shares in a ship may only be sold by Bill of Sale,

ibid., s.24. It is not necessary to make an actual seizure of the ship for the shares to be sold and especially where the execution debtor owns part of the shares only. For transfer by Order of the Court, see s.29.

Soldiers, Sailors and Airmen

By the Army Act, 1955, the Air Force Act, 1955 and the Naval Discipline Act, 1957 the arms, ammunition, equipment, instruments and clothing used for service purposes are exempt from seizure.

Statutory Allowance

See the comments at the beginning of this chapter.

Tools of Trade

In deciding if an item is "an implement of trade", Horridge, J stated, when considering if testimonials, letters of introduction and other documents fell within the exempt category, "I am clearly of the opinion that these documents are not "tools of his trade" within the exception in s.38 of the Act (Bankruptcy Act, 1914, now repealed). That exception was intended for the protection of workmen so that they might not be prevented from earning a livelihood with the implements of their trade", (*Re Sherman* (1915) 32 TLR 231).

A corporate entity may not claim the benefit of the exemption, neither may a partnership firm.

A cab was considered an "implement of trade" and the execution issued against the cab-driver frustrated as a

result. (*Lavell v. Richings* (1906) 1 KB 480), but, in
Addison v. Shepherd (1908) 2 KB 118, samples held by
a commercial traveller were not considered to be
"implements of trade". In *Toseland Building Supplies Ltd
v. Bishop* (1993) (*supra*), the debtor's claim concerned a
JCB excavator and the claim was defeated only because
the debtor occasionally allowed his employee to operate
the machine when he was unable to do so himself. He
could not show that the machine was for his own
exclusive personal use. The term "necessary" in s.138
(3A)(a) & (b), Supreme Court Act 1981 has not yet, so far
as we are aware, been defined in this context by the
Court. See also the discussion at the commencement of
this chapter.

Stolen Goods

If the Officer seizes and sells goods which subsequently
prove to have been stolen, the title acquired by the
purchaser may be invalidated. This was confirmed by the
Court of Appeal in *National Employers Mutual General
Insurance Association Limited v. Jones, The Independent,*
March 31, 1987, where the final purchaser in a chain of
buyers of a motor car which had been stolen could not
rely on s.25 of the Sale of Goods Act, 1979 to resist the
claim of the original owner from whom the car had been
stolen. No person may pass on a better title to goods than
he had himself.

CHAPTER 5

Walking Possession

In executing a writ of *fi:fa*, it is the duty of the Officer to maintain physical possession of the effects he has seized. However the practice of entering into "walking possession" has not only become acceptable but has been encouraged to prevent unnecessary cost, inconvenience and interference falling upon the debtor.

In 1929, the Lord Chancellor's Department issued a circular to all Registrars and High Bailiffs (No.6 of 1929) which included:

> "The Lord Chancellor considers it is to the public advantage that walking possession should be adopted by High Bailiffs to the utmost possible extent, goods being removed or a possession man being put into close possession only in cases where it is considered that course is necessary to safeguard the goods ... The decision regarding the individual cases in which Walking Possession can be adopted with reasonable safety and at what intervals it is necessary in such cases for a Bailiff or possession man to visit the premises will of course continue to be matters within the discretion of the High Bailiff."

In the County Court the practice grew of attending at the debtor's premises, seizing and listing the goods and returning only to ensure safety or to arrange removal and sale. The form of the agreement which the debtor should sign follows that shown in County Court Forms, N334. It records that a seizure has been made, that the Bailiff may return to inspect or remove the goods, that the debtor requests that a possession man is not left on the premises and that the debtor undertakes to inform any other bailiff or Sheriff's Officer who attends, of the seizure.

The practice of walking possession was finally acknowledged in the High Court by the inclusion of the Walking Possession Agreement in the Sheriff's Fees Amendment Order, 1956. A copy of that agreement is given at the end of this chapter.

It is not necessary for the form to be signed by the debtor, a signature by any responsible person at the premises is acceptable (*National Commercial Bank of Scotland Ltd v. Arcam Demolition and Construction Ltd* (1966) 2 QB 593).

Having obtained walking possession, and having obtained an agreement to re-enter by force if necessary, is evidence of seizure (*Watson v. Murray* (1955) 2 QB 1), but the absence of such an agreement is not evidence that seizure did not take place (*Lloyds & Scottish Finance Ltd v. Modern Cars & Caravans (Kingston) Ltd* (1964) 2 All ER 732).

A walking possession agreement is not binding against an owner of goods who knows nothing of the agreement and who is unaware of the distraint or levy and who removes his own goods (*Abingdon RDC v. O'Gorman* (1968), 2 QB 811).

Following Goods

The duty of the Sheriff to record the time and date of the lodgment of the writ is not only to establish priority, the debtor's effects are bound in his hands from that time and title may only be transferred to a bona fide purchaser for valuable consideration.

However, this relates only to where the writ remains in the Sheriff's hands and remains unexecuted. Once a seizure has been made, a third party may not acquire an unencumbered title even if a sale took place for valuable consideration and without the purchaser having knowledge of the *fi:fa*. The Officer may follow and remove those goods to raise the amount due under the writ (*Lloyds & Scottish Finance Ltd v. Modern Cars & Caravans (Kingston) Ltd* (1964) *supra*).

Further Attendances

There is no requirement to attend on a regular basis or on specified occasions but there is a requirement to ensure that the parties involved are aware that a seizure has been made. Whether the goods have been abandoned is a question of fact, but the details of each case must be considered on its merits (*Bagshaws Ltd v. Deacon* (1898) 2 QB 173). This decision was reached before the practice of walking possession had become common but remains valid.

To assist the Officer in defending any action, either a copy of the walking possession agreement or similar document detailing the execution and stating that a seizure has been made should be left at the debtor's premises. Whilst it may be ideal to attach that notice to the building for public view, it would be impractical as the debtor could merely remove it from sight. Examples of both forms are given at the end of this chapter.

Failure to obtain an agreement

Where the Sheriff is unable to obtain a signed walking possession agreement, either because the debtor refuses to sign or for some other reason, his duty is to remove the goods as soon as is practicable, or, at very least, inspect the goods at frequent intervals, daily if possible. If he does not do so, the Court will likely hold that possession of the goods has been abandoned and in that case the debtor will be under no penalty if he disposes of them.

No Limit on Possession

There is no requirement to quit possession after a specified length of time but any delay can only be at the request of both parties. Certainly, if any other bailiff or creditor wishes to proceed under a later warrant or distress, the Officer must invite the execution creditor to instruct the Sheriff to proceed immediately or to withdraw.

Continual Possession

Where writs are issued against the same property by more than one judgment creditor, separate seizures are not necessary, one seizure enuring for the benefit of all (*Re Henderson, ex parte Shaw* (1884) WN 60; *Re Hille* (1897) WN 20, and see notes to O.47, r.2(2) in *Supreme Court Practice*).

As mentioned in the section PRIORITY, if the Sheriff is already in possession and a second writ is delivered, the Sheriff is considered to have seized under the second writ as soon as it is received.

Naturally, it is advisable for the Officer to inform the debtor of this later writ. Yet it appears that only one walking possession form is required. However, if the value of the effects is more than sufficient to satisfy the first execution, a further seizure should be made under the later warrant. In such circumstances a second seizure fee has been allowed on taxation.

Insurance

There is no obligation to insure effects which remain in the control and custody of the debtor. Where effects are in the control and custody of the Officer, for example where the debtor has vacated the premises and a sale is to be conducted on the premises, the Officer may consider either seeking insurance cover or ensuring that regular visits are made to confirm the safety of the goods. (See also *Mather*, 3rd edn, p.119).

Where effects are removed, all risks insurance should be obtained in case of damage or loss during transit or whilst awaiting sale. It may be that the Officer or his agents already have such cover under existing policies but care must be taken that the insured value is adequate and that specialized items are included.

Form of Walking Possession Agreement as in Sheriff's Fees Amendment Order, 1956

In the High Court of Justice
..............................Division

Between   ....Plaintiff

and   ....Defendant

To the Sheriff of ....

    I hereby request that you will not leave a possession man on my premises in close possession of the goods which you have seized under the writ of execution issued in this action.
    If this convenience is allowed to me, I undertake, pending the withdrawal or satisfaction of the writ:-

a) not to remove the said goods or any part thereof nor to permit their removal by any person not authorised by you in that behalf;

b) to inform any person who may visit my premises for the purpose of levying execution or distress that you are already in possession of my goods under the above writ;

c) to notify you immediately at your office of any such visit.

    And I authorize you, or any of your Officers, pending withdrawal or satisfaction of the above writ, to re-enter my premises at any time and as often as you may consider necessary for the purpose of inspecting the said goods or completing the execution of the writ.

Dated this .... day of ....19....

.... Judgment Debtor

Suggested Form which may be left
at the Debtor's premises

In the High Court of Justice

...............................Division

Between   ....Plaintiff
and   ....Defendant

Address of premises ....

This notice is left by an Officer of the Sheriff who has seized the goods and chattels at this address under a High Court warrant. To ascertain the amount that must be paid by Banker's Draft, Postal Orders or Money Orders (no cheques) to satisfy the judgment and costs please communicate immediately with the Sheriff's Officers.

If the judgment is not satisfied, sufficient of the goods so seized will be removed and sold at public auction to recover the debt and all costs incurred.

If any of the goods are the property of Third Parties or on Hire Purchase or Rental you must notify the owners AND the Sheriff's Officers.

Owners must make a written claim specifying the goods claimed and if such claim is not admitted by the creditor, the Sheriff will ask the Court to decide whether such goods can be released.

Until the Judgment debt and all costs are paid the goods remain in the custody of the Sheriff and must not be sold or removed or taken by third parties without the prior authority of the Sheriff's Officers.

For the Sheriff's Officers
(name, address and reference)

(Give details of the judgment debt, costs, interest etc.)

CHAPTER 6

Claims & Interpleader

Introduction

In levying under the Sheriff's Warrant, an Officer will frequently meet a claim by a third party. The claim may be made by a trade supplier, finance company, or by a member of the judgment debtor's family ("the claimant"). The claim will be to the goods seized or intended to be seized ("the goods") under the warrant. It may say only that some or all these goods do not belong to the judgment debtor but belong to the claimant. These goods cannot be sold in satisfaction of the writ of execution until an Order is obtained from the Court allowing the Sheriff to do so.

Third party claims need to be managed as efficiently as possible. Once the Officer has received a claim he must deal with it according to the Rules of the Supreme Court, (the Rules). Interpleader proceedings in the High Court are dealt with under RSC Order 17 : Interpleader.

Position of the Sheriff

The Sheriff stands in the midst of all the competing interests of execution creditor and claimant. He is a neutral party, and this neutrality gives him a unique position to oversee the management of the claim. Therefore although an Officer is required to see if there is a third party claim, he is not required to go beyond asking if there is a claim. Nor is he obliged to help a claimant in formulating a claim. It is for the claimant to know what it is he claims. A wife may be able to write a claim to ownership of items in the matrimonial home. However, a tradesman may not be able to itemise every item of stock in a warehouse or shop.

This chapter is written on the basis that a claim is made, and a decision from the Court will be required.

However not every claim will be made in writing, and not every claim will result in Interpleader proceedings being issued. These problems are dealt with below by using the following stages after a claim is received:

Stage 1 :   Form of claim and the need to investigate
Stage 2 :   Types of claim and what to look for
Stage 3 :   Action to be taken on receipt of a third party claim
Stage 4 :   Action to be taken if the claim is admitted
Stage 5 :   Action to be taken if claim disputed
Stage 6 :   Issuing the interpleader summons
Stage 7 :   Serving the interpleader summons
Stage 8 :   Preparing for the first hearing
Stage 9 :   The claimant's affidavit
Stage 10 :   The first hearing
Stage 11 :   Working through directions - points to note
Stage 12 :   The final hearing and next steps
Stage 13 :   Payment of the sheriff's interpleader costs and charges

Stage 1 : Form of Claim and the Need to Investigate

Form of Claim

The Officer will need to obtain a claim in writing if the Sheriff is eventually to seek interpleader relief. The levy notice appearing on p.69 puts a potential claimant on notice of the need for a written claim, and highlights the possibility of an application to the Court.

Oral Claims and the Need to Investigate

An oral claim is not sufficient to enable a Sheriff to seek interpleader relief (see Stage 5 below). However, an oral claim must be fully investigated. If such a claim is not fully investigated, and the goods are subsequently sold, the Sheriff will not be able to protect himself from any possible legal action being brought by the claimant (but see Stage 12 - the final order). In *Observer Ltd v. Gordon* (1983) 2 All ER 945, the Sheriff seized and sold pianos removed from the judgment debtor's work rooms. The judgment debtor had died and all the pianos were subject to third party claims from persons who had left the pianos with her for repair. The Sheriff was unaware of the third party claims which only came to light after the pianos had been sold. In that case, the interpleader concerned the proceeds of sale which were still in the hands of the Sheriff.

Debtors will often be reluctant to reveal whether the goods are subject to a third party claim. They will not want their trading suppliers or other creditors to be made aware of the judgment against them. Nevertheless, the Officer must take all reasonable steps to ensure that the assets seized are those of the debtor. Even if the debtor signs a walking possession agreement the Officer should ask the debtor if there are any claims.

The Officer can also make inquiries of such authorities as the Driver and Vehicle Licensing Agency, and H.P. Information Ltd and other registers that record ownership of goods.

Investigation of Merits

The Officer must not attempt to investigate the merits of a claim however bad they may appear. Any action which interferes with the Court's ability to decide the merits of the claim may affect the Sheriff's right to seek interpleader relief (*Crump v. Day* (1847) 4 CB 760).

Referral of Claim to Execution Creditor

As a matter of good practice, it is wise to inform the execution creditor of the likelihood of a third party claim even if it is not made in writing. It may be that the execution creditor has information, or can make further inquiries about the third party from information held on his file. A decision can then be made as to whether to continue with the execution of the warrant. Information about the goods claimed, the safety of the goods and the possible cost involved of seeking interpleader relief should all be highlighted to the execution creditor as early as possible. Again, matters of cost will be significant factors in whether the execution creditor decides to dispute the claim.

Claims in Writing

To comply with RSC, O.17, r.2, the requirements of a valid form of claim can be summarized as follows:

> the claim should be in writing;
>
> it should be addressed to the Sheriff or to the Officer;
>
> it must state the name and address of the claimant (which becomes the claimant's address for service of any interpleader summons);
>
> it must be dated;
>
> the claimant must be identified. It is a requirement under the Companies Act 1985 that a company must publish certain information on its correspondence (including the company name and its registration number);
>
> it should make a positive statement as to ownership of the goods;
>
> the items claimed should be specifically identified;
>
> but, the claim need not necessarily be signed (see *J.P.R. Plastics Ltd v. Gordon Rossall Plastics Ltd, (Hexa Pen Co. Ltd, Claimants)* (1950) 1 All ER 241, DC).

Claims Not in Valid Form

A claim which is not made in accordance with the Rules, (ie, it does not contain all the information outlined above) is not a valid claim and the Sheriff cannot interplead until it is in the required form. The Officer should obtain a valid claim as soon as possible.

Stage 2 : Types of Claim and What to Look For

Types of Claims

Claims to "goods taken, or intended to be taken, in execution" - ie, there must have been an actual seizure or an intention of the Sheriff to seize (see RSC, O.17/1/7), will vary widely. The most common claims are those by a husband or wife, or by an associated company of the judgment debtor company. Other claims that may be received are from Hire Purchase companies and claims from suppliers who have sold goods to a debtor while retaining title until paid (*Romalpa* agreements). Points to note on different types of claim include the following:

Joint Ownership

Goods claimed by the debtor and others jointly, or as "tenants in common", can be sold by the Sheriff. The claims of the co-owners can be the subject of interpleader proceedings and the Court will decide how the proceeds of sale are to be distributed (*Farrar v. Beswick* (1836) 1 M & W 682; *Mayhew v. Herrick* (1849) 7 CB 229).

Partnerships

Disputes as to partnership property, or whether a partnership exists, can both be the subject of interpleader proceedings (see the Partnership Act 1890, s.23 (as amended); *Peake v. Carter* (1916) 1 KB 652 at 655, CA *per* Swinfen Eady LJ).

Bills of Sale

A "bill of sale" is a written document by which one party transfers property in goods or chattels to another. Usually a bill of sale is only required where the party transferring the goods or chattels intends to retain possession after transferring the items to the new owner.

Legislation relating to bills of sale is contained in the Bills of Sale Acts 1878 and 1882. The legislation was designed to balance the rights of creditor and debtor resulting in strict registration and attestation provisions. Bills of sale therefore have to be registered in the Bills of Sale Register which is located in the Filing Department of the Central Office at the Royal Courts of Justice, Strand, London WC2A 2LL.

If a claimant says that he owns the goods by virtue of a bill of sale he must provide the Court with evidence of registration according to the statutory procedures.

Hire Purchase

The Officer should ask to see a copy of the HP agreement and should submit this to the execution creditor as soon as possible for consideration. Officers should be careful to distinguish between Hire Purchase and Credit Sale agreements.

Credit Sale Agreements

A credit sale agreement will not give rise to a valid claim to goods as the property in the goods passes on signing the agreement.

Landlords

The Sheriff is prohibited from removing goods from premises where he has notice from a landlord that rent is owing. By virtue of s.1 of the Landlord & Tenant Act 1709, he cannot remove the goods until the rent owing - which may be up to one year's arrears - has been paid.

If the Sheriff attempts to remove and sell the goods before the rent is paid, the landlord can bring an action against him under the statute.

When the Sheriff is met with a claim from the landlord for unpaid rent, he cannot interplead (see *Clarke v. Lord* (1833) 2 Dowl PC 55,227; *Bateman v. Farnsworth* (1860) 2 LT 390).

The 1709 Act only applies to tenancies existing at the time of seizure by the Sheriff (*Risley v. Ryle* (1842) 10 M & W 101). Therefore if at the date of seizure the tenancy has been determined the Sheriff must not pay the landlord any arrears (*Hodgson v. Gascoigne* (1821) 5 B & Ald 88).

If the landlord makes a claim to goods in the premises (without reference to rent) then the claim should be dealt with in the usual way.

See ch.8 for a full discussion of Landlord's Claim for Rent.

Suppliers of Goods Subject to Reservation of Title Clauses ("Romalpa Agreements")

Agreements containing reservation of title clauses are more commonly known as "Romalpa" agreements following the case of *Aluminium Industrie Vaasen v. Romalpa Aluminium* (1976) 2 All ER 552.

Under the Sale of Goods Act 1979, retention of title

clauses provide that although goods may be delivered to the buyer, property does not pass in those goods until the conditions imposed by the seller relating to disposal are fulfilled (see Sale of Goods Act (1979) s.19(1)).

If a claim is made by a seller that the goods are subject to a retention of title clause, the Officer should ask to see a copy of the agreement and contract. This should be submitted to the execution creditor for him to admit or dispute.

Interesting points to note include:

If title passes, but will pass back to the seller, for example on the appointment of a receiver, a charge will have been created. In these circumstances the title will have passed and the retention of title clause will not be effective.

If the goods supplied under the contract are indistinguishable from other goods and stock held by the debtor then title to the goods supplied will be lost (see *Border (UK) Ltd v. Scottish Timber Products Ltd* (1979) 3 All ER 961).

Administrative Receivers / Debenture Holders

A claim by a debenture holder can be the subject of interpleader proceedings if, for example, the validity of the receiver's appointment is disputed. The Officer should therefore seek a copy of the debenture holder's agreement. This should be submitted to the execution creditor for a decision on whether the claim should be admitted or disputed.

The receiver is simply a third party and does not enjoy any particular privilege as against the Sheriff. He is not in the same position as a liquidator and he cannot call on the Sheriff to surrender goods (see Insolvency Act, 1986, ss.28-49).

His claim to control or custody of the goods must follow the form of any other claim.

A receiver may not recover monies held by the Sheriff as they do not constitute monies of the debtor (*Robinson v. Burnell's Vienna Bakery Co. Ltd* (1904) KB 624).

It should be noted that where a charge under a debenture agreement crystallizes by the valid appointment of a receiver before the completion of the execution (ie, by seizure and sale of the goods) then the rights of the debenture holder will take priority over those of the execution creditor, (see *Re Standard Manufacturing Co.* (1891) 1 Ch 627, CA; *Re Opera Limited* (1891) 3 Ch 260, CA; and see *Taunton v. Sheriff of Warwickshire* (1895) 2 Ch 319, CA; *Evans v. Rival Granite Quarries Ltd* (1910) 2 KB 979, CA; *Robinson v. Burnell's Vienna Bakery Co. Ltd* (1904) 2 KB 624; *Heaton and Dugard Ltd v. Cutting Bros Ltd* (1925) 1 KB 655, DC).

Insolvency - Claims by Liquidators

Insolvency is fully dealt with in ch.7. Generally, if a judgment debtor (be it an individual or company) becomes insolvent during the interpleader proceedings then the Sheriff will not have completed the execution against the goods by seizure and sale, and the execution creditor will not be able to retain the benefit of the execution.

In general, the Sheriff may not interplead on a claim by a liquidator because he has a statutory duty to him. The only grounds that may perhaps be valid for such a procedure appear to be where the creditor disputes the validity of the liquidator's appointment.

The Sheriff must keep the execution creditor and claimant fully informed about the possibility of any insolvency even if the required notice under the Insolvency Act has not been served.

Stage 3 : Receipt of Claim (see RSC, O.17, r.2)

On receipt of a claim the Officer must forward it to the execution creditor or his solicitors. A decision needs to be made whether to admit or dispute the claim. The decision must be made within seven days of receiving the notice from the Sheriff. The seven day period is calculated in accordance with RSC, O.3, r.2.

Any clear written notice sent by the Sheriff to the execution creditor enclosing a copy of the claim will suffice. The Sheriff's right to claim interpleader relief is conditional upon such a notice being given (*Dalton v. Furness* (1866) 35 Beav 461).

For a form of notice that invites the execution creditor to admit or dispute see the appendix to this chapter.

As a matter of good practice, the sending of the form and the seven day period should be noted and reviewed. There is nothing in the rules to prevent an Officer faxing the notice and the copy claim to the execution creditor to help speed up the decision on whether the claim is disputed.

If the Officer has not already done so, he should give the execution creditor as much information as possible about the goods, and their likely value at an auction sale. The execution creditor and his solicitor will welcome any information to help in deciding whether it is worth disputing the claim in the light of:

(a)   Sheriff's charges;

(b) Sheriff's costs of the interpleader proceedings;

(c) out of pocket expenses incurred by the Officers such as removal and storage costs.

Notice to Sheriff

The execution creditor must respond to the Sheriff within seven days of receiving notice of a claim with the decision whether to admit or dispute that claim. (RSC, O.17, r.2(2)).

Stage 4 : Action to be Taken if the Claim is Admitted

Order for No Action

If the decision is made to admit the claim the Sheriff must withdraw from possession of the goods claimed. The Sheriff may apply to the court for an order "restraining the bringing of an action against him for or in respect of his having taken possession of the goods" (RSC, O.17, r.2(4)). If the Sheriff wishes to apply *he should do so promptly.*

The Officer should always consider whether an application for interpleader relief should be made.

Conduct

The Sheriff's conduct and that of his Officers will have a direct bearing on whether such an order can be granted (see *Cave v. Capel* (1954) 1 QB 367 at 369-370, and also *Neumann v. Bakeaway Ltd (Ghotli, Claimant)* (1983) 2

All ER 935 at 942)).

The Court will not grant an order protecting the Sheriff from any future action by the claimant where it appears:

(a) the claimant has a "real grievance" against the Sheriff (see *Cave v. Capel* (1954) *supra*); or

(b) the Sheriff fails to withdraw from possession of the goods after receiving the notice from the execution creditor admitting the claim (see *Sodeau v. Shorey* (1896) 74 LT 240 CA).

No Notice from Execution Creditor

Furthermore, without any notice from the execution creditor admitting the claim, the Sheriff will be at risk if he:

(a) withdraws without seizure (*Holton v. Guntrip* (1837) 6 Dowl 130); or

(b) seizes and then withdraws (*Crump v. Day* (1847) 4 CB 760); or

(c) delivers up the goods or some of them (*Braine v. Hunt* (1843) 2 Dowl 391); or

(d) pays over the proceeds to the claimant or to the execution creditor (*Anderson v. Calloway* (1832) 1 Dowl 636; *Scott v. Lewis* (1835) 4 Dowl 259); or

(e) relinquishes possession of the goods so that they are no longer in the custody of the law and may be available to be distrained upon for rent (see *Cropper v. Warner* (1883) Cab & El 152).

Therefore the Sheriff must stay in possession until he receives written instructions from the execution creditor that the claim is admitted. Without a decision he should consider issuing interpleader proceedings for his own protection after the expiry of the seven day period.

Liability for Sheriff's Charges

The execution creditor is only liable for the Sheriff's fees and expenses incurred before the Sheriff received the notice admitting the claim (see RSC, O.17, r.2(2)). But if after the issue, and before the return day of an interpleader summons, the execution creditor admits the claim, or the claimant withdraws the claim, the Court may make any order as to costs or any other matter as it thinks just (RSC, O.17, r.8).

Stage 5 : Action to be Taken if Claim Disputed

If the claim is disputed or no instructions are received from the execution creditor within the seven day period, then provided the claim has not been withdrawn by the claimant, the Sheriff may apply to the Court for interpleader relief. In applying to the Court for "relief" the Sheriff must be, or expect to be, sued. The Court will be asked to decide, on the evidence before it, whether the claimant owns

> "any money, goods or chattels taken, or intended to be taken, by a Sheriff in execution ... or to the proceeds or value of any such goods or chattels" (RSC O.17, r.1(1)(b)).

It is important to note the three conditions that must exist before the application can be made:

(a)   the Sheriff or Officer claims no interest in the goods other than for charges or costs. Any interest must be disclosed to the Court at the first hearing of the interpleader summons (see RSC, O.17, r. 3(4)), and;

(b)   the Sheriff or Officer has not colluded (meaning that the Sheriff has not "played on the same side" as one of the claimants (see *Fredericks and Pelhams Timber Buildings v. Wilkins (Read, Claimant)* (1971) 3 All ER 545 at 551) and;

(c)   the Sheriff is willing to pay the proceeds or transfer the goods into court, or to dispose of those goods following any direction given by the Court.

Time Period to Begin Proceedings

The application should be made as quickly as possible. If the Sheriff does not act promptly, he may be refused interpleader relief, or be penalized on costs (*Cook v. Allen* (1833) 2 L.J.Ex 199).

Any claimant who begins any action against the Sheriff before giving the Sheriff an opportunity to interplead may also be penalized on costs (*Hilliard v. Hanson* (1882) 31 WR 151).

Information Needed To Make Application

The Officer should forward all the relevant documents to the Sheriff's solicitor for the issue and conduct of the interpleader summons. The original letter of claim together with the following information should be submitted:

1. Priority date of writ: are there prior or subsequent warrants?
2. Levy date:
3. Levy address: indicate whether this is a private or business address.
4. Levy amount: as *per* the writ of execution.
5. WP form: whether signed and status of signatory.
6. Description of goods: (see 8 below). .
7. Value of goods: this should include factors which may affect sale price and whether the Sheriff should apply to sell by private treaty.
8. Inventory: is the claimant still trading? should photographs be taken to identify items that are subject of the claim?
9. Any search result: DVLA/HPI.
10. Date claim received:
11. Claim disputed: any reason for delay should be highlighted.
12. Up-to date Sheriff's charges: figure projected for the total amount of charges.

Stage 6 : Issuing the Interpleader Summons

Form of Summons

For a form of summons see Form No.1 in the appendix to this chapter. The wording requires the claimant to appear and state the nature and particulars of the claim by preparing an affidavit which should be served on the execution creditor and the Sheriff. Frequently claimants do not serve their affidavits as required by the direction in the summons until ordered to do so by the Court.

More Than One Claimant

It is possible to have more than one claimant in interpleader proceedings. If it appears likely that there will be more than one claim it is worth considering how best to present the situation to the Court.

Acknowledgment of Summons

The claimant does not have to acknowledge service of the summons.

Venue For Interpleader Proceedings

The rules for where the proceedings should be issued can be summarized as follows: (see RSC, O.17, r.4)

(a)   If the "main" action (ie, the action between the creditor and debtor) is proceeding in the Royal Courts of Justice in the Strand, London, then the Sheriff should apply to a Master.

(b)   If the writ of execution has been or is being levied in the district of a district registry, the Sheriff may apply to either a Master or a District Judge of that particular district registry.

(c)   If the "main" action is proceeding in a district registry, the Sheriff should apply to the District Judge of that registry.

(d)   If the writ of execution has been or is being levied in the district of some other district registry or outside the jurisdiction of a district registry, the Sheriff should apply to:

(i)   the District Judge of the district registry where the "main" action is proceeding; or

(ii)   the District Judge of the district registry where execution is being levied; or

(iii)   to a Master of the High Court as the case may be.

If the "main action" is proceeding in the Admiralty Court then the application is made to the Admiralty Registrar. Similarly in the Family Division, the application is made to the District Judge.

Generally it will be more convenient to issue proceedings in the court nearest to where the goods are located.

Speed of Application

The application must be made as quickly as possible. The goods remain, throughout the application, in the custody of the law and cannot be released until a final order is made in the proceedings. The Court appreciates the urgency of the application and will generally arrange a very early appointment for the first return of the interpleader summons.

Extension of Validity of Writ of Execution

Once an interpleader summons is issued, the validity of the writ of execution is automatically extended for a period of 12 months from the date of the final order in the proceedings (see RSC, O.46, r.8(6)).

Effect on Execution

The issue of the interpleader summons does not itself stay
further proceedings in respect of the goods claimed but
the summons asks for such a stay. The Court may grant
a stay under RSC, O.17, r.7. However no action should
be taken in relation to the goods once the summons has
been issued. If the Officer considers that

(a)   the goods are at risk of removal; and
(b)   the claimant or debtor refuses to sign a walking
      possession agreement acknowledging seizure

then the Officer should inform the Sheriff's solicitor
immediately.

An application should then be made to the Court for
an order that the Sheriff "have leave to remove the goods
to a place of safety forthwith". In making the application
the Sheriff's solicitor will need to inform the Court why
the Officer believes that the goods are at risk. The failure
to sign a walking possession agreement is evidence that
a risk exists.

Stage 7 : Serving the Interpleader Summons

Time Allowed for Service of the Summons

The interpleader summons must be served at least 14
days before the first hearing date of the interpleader
proceedings.

Address for Service Upon Claimant

The claimant's address for service will be the address
appearing on the notice of claim (RSC, O.17 r.2(1)).

Method of Service

Service of the interpleader summons on both parties is governed by the Rules. However it is worth considering how best to serve the summons on the claimant and a combination of the following methods might be preferable:

(a)   leaving a copy of the summons at the claimant's address for service; and/or

(b)   meeting the claimant in person and handing him a copy of the summons; and/or

(c)   posting it to the claimant (see RSC. O.65, r.5); and/or

(d)   leaving it at a document exchange where appropriate.

In any event, the method, date and time of service should be recorded in case the Sheriff is asked to prepare an Affidavit of Service of the summons on the parties.

Service Outside the Jurisdiction

Occasionally the Officer will be told that a claim will be made by a person or company who is outside the jurisdiction of the High Court (ie, England and Wales). If such a claim is received, the Sheriff's solicitor must seek leave from the Court to serve the summons outside the jurisdiction. An affidavit will be needed which will exhibit the original letter of claim (see RSC, O.11, r.9).

If the claimant has solicitors within the jurisdiction then the need for leave to serve the interpleader summons outside the jurisdiction may be overcome.

The Debtor

The debtor is not a party to the interpleader proceedings, subject to any order of the Court to the contrary.

Stage Eight : Preparing for the First Hearing

If possible, the Sheriff needs an order at the earliest opportunity to determine whether he should execute the warrant or should withdraw from possession of the third party's goods. The Sheriff's solicitor can probably anticipate what orders will be needed to deal with the interpleader issue. Certainly the aim should be to obtain as many directions as possible to deal with the proceedings at the first return. Much will depend on whether the claimant has prepared an affidavit and, whether he has had the benefit of legal advice.

The Sheriff's Officer's Report

To prepare for the hearing the Sheriff's solicitor will need to have all the relevant facts available regarding the execution of the warrant and the claim (see Stage 5 for the information which is needed initially). Information should be updated to take account of changes in fees and costs since the summons was issued and also any changes in relation to the goods or levels of stock which have taken place.

The Sheriff's Inventory

The claimant has to prove ownership of the goods to the

satisfaction of the Court.

Claimants often believe they can use the Sheriff's inventory to help prepare their affidavit. But a claimant cannot call on the Sheriff for particulars of the goods, to help in the preparation of the claim (see *Bauly v. Crook* (1891) 65 L.T.377 and RSC, O.17/3/3).

The Court may order the Sheriff to produce an inventory to be used in the proceedings and to provide the parties with a copy of it. The inventory provided could include photographs to help the parties to visualize the goods.

Where goods seized are claimed, the Sheriff should not provide a copy of the inventory to one side only (see *Fredericks and Pelhams Timber Buildings v. Wilkins (Read, Claimant)* (1971) 3 All ER 545 at 546-551).

The preparation of an inventory is a step in the execution for which the Sheriff can charge the prescribed fee under the Sheriff's Fee Order.

Up-to-date Information on Safety of the Goods

As a matter of good practice, the Officer ought to attend and check on the safety of the goods as often as possible while interpleader proceedings are in progress. He should inform the execution creditor and Sheriff's solicitor as to the pattern of attendance and seek agreement that this is acceptable.

A signature to a walking possession agreement cannot be relied upon to ensure that the goods remain at a particular address. The Officer must remain vigilant, and if he considers the goods are at risk, then a decision will have to be made on whether to take the goods into close possession. The Officer must keep the execution creditor and Sheriff's solicitor fully informed regarding any possible risk to the safety of the goods. If it is necessary to take the goods into custody, information about removal and storage charges should be given.

Up-to-date Information on Sheriff's Charges

Up-to-date information about costs and charges is very important particularly if the value of the goods is low or difficult to gauge. The execution creditor can make an informed choice about whether to continue to dispute the claim.

The Sheriff's solicitor should always keep up-to-date information about the costs on file. This may be useful if the parties want to negotiate a settlement.

Stage 9 : The Claimant's Affidavit

The Requirement for an Affidavit from the Claimant

A claimant should, within 14 days of receiving the interpleader summons, swear and file an affidavit in support of his claim (see RSC, O.17, r.3(6)). Under the Rules, the interpleader summons must notify the claimant of this requirement (see RSC, O.17 r.3(7)). It is open to a claimant to attend the hearing, without an affidavit, on the basis that he objects to an irregularity in the proceedings or to argue that the Sheriff has no right to interpleader relief (see RSC, O.17/5/1).

The Content of the Claimant's Affidavit

The affidavit should be sufficiently precise to:

(a) enable the execution creditor (and any opposing claimant) to decide whether to continue to dispute the claim; and

(b) allow the Court to make any orders in the proceedings (see *Powell v. Lock* (1835) 3 A & E 315).

A properly prepared affidavit served by the claimant may eventually save expense in the proceedings. The affidavit ought to relate to the Sheriff's inventory, although the claimant will not have been allowed to use the inventory in preparing the affidavit.

If any items are omitted from the affidavit then those items may be subject to a claim barred order; although the claimant may make submissions to the Court as to why those items were omitted and the Court may then make further directions.

Affidavits from Other Parties

Neither the Sheriff nor the execution creditor are required to make an affidavit. An execution creditor may seek leave to serve an affidavit in reply to the claimant's affidavit.

Stage 10 : The First Hearing

Attendance by the Claimant

The claimant must appear at the hearing personally or be represented by a solicitor (see RSC, O.17, r.5(1)). A company can only be represented by a solicitor (see RSC, O.5/6/2).

Possible Orders

These can be summarized as follows:

An Order Barring the Claim -

This will be made if the claimant fails to attend the hearing and has no legal representation (see RSC, O.17/5/3) but the Court does not have power to make an order against a claimant who actually appears and makes out some sort of claim however "nebulous" (see *J.R.P. Plastics Limited v. Gordon Rossall Plastics Limited (Hexa Pen Co. Limited, Claimants)* (1950) 1 All ER 241 DC).

If the claim is barred in the absence of the claimant, the Sheriff will usually be required to swear an affidavit of service which will exhibit the interpleader summons and will state the date and time the summons was posted, or the circumstances of service of the document on the claimant.

Sheriff Ordered to Withdraw

Occasionally the claimant will have prepared an affidavit, or there will be some other circumstances which will lead the execution creditor to decide to admit the claim. An order should not be made by the Court allowing the claimant's claim unless the execution creditor consents or he has had a chance to cross examine the claimant at a hearing and there has been discovery of documents prior to that hearing (see *P.B.J. Davies Manufacturing Co. Limited v. Fahn (Claimant)* (1967) 1 WLR 1059).

Claimant Attends Hearing but has not Prepared an Affidavit

The Court can make an order requiring the claimant to serve an affidavit. It may make an "unless" order, so that if the claimant fails to comply by a particular date, the claim will be barred. An "unless" order requires careful monitoring by the Sheriff's solicitor and Officer.

Discovery and Inspection of Documents

The claimant may be ordered to prepare a list as required under RSC O.24: Discovery, that may or may not be ordered to be verified by affidavit.

Issue to be Adjourned for Summary Disposal on a Date to be Fixed

As a general guide a summary disposal will be ordered in straightforward cases, particularly where the interpleader issue must be dealt with quickly, when for example, the goods are perishable.

Trial of an Issue

Where the case involves valuable goods or difficult questions of law, then the Master will direct "the Trial of an Issue". The important point to note here is that an appeal from the decision of a Master made by summary disposal lies to the Judge in chambers. But an appeal from the decision of the Master following the trial of an issue lies directly to the Court of Appeal.

Refer the Matter to the Judge

In Chancery proceedings there is no appeal as such from the Master's decision but the Master will adjourn the summons to a Judge in chambers on the application of either party.

Transfer the Proceedings to the County Court

The High Court must transfer the proceedings to a County Court if it considers it appropriate. In doing so, it must take into account the convenience of the parties, the facts of the case, and any likely savings in costs (see generally s.40, County Courts Act 1984). If the proceedings are transferred, then they are subject to the procedural rules of the County Court (CCR) and in particular CCR O.16, r.7.

Dispute to be Referred to Arbitration

Such disputes can only be referred if all the claimants are party to an arbitration agreement.

Sale of Goods

This may be ordered if:

(a)   it will save costs and charges (see RSC O. 17/5/8); or

(b)   if the claimant alleges he is entitled to the goods under a Bill of Sale by way of security for a debt (see RSC, O.17, r.6).

Dealing with Particular Circumstances

During the conduct of the interpleader, the court may make orders for the safety of the goods, for the insurance and custody of the goods, for payment of costs such as storage, to allow the claimant to purchase the interest of the debtor from the Sheriff and any other orders that may be considered relevant under its general powers in RSC, O.17, r.8. The Sheriff's solicitor should inform the Court of all the circumstances of the case using the information provided by the Officer and the parties, and ask the Court to make additional appropriate orders.

Costs

If directions are made, then the issue of the Sheriff's costs is usually "reserved" and costs will continue to be reserved until the final order (see Stage 12 below).

Liberty to Restore

The Sheriff seeks an order allowing the summons to be restored for further directions should this prove necessary - if the interpleader is ongoing this should be a standard request to the Master.

A form of Order setting out directions for the service of an affidavit by the claimant and accompanying directions appears as Form No.4 in the appendix to this chapter.

No Attendance at the Hearing by Either of the Parties

If the execution creditor does not attend the hearing and does not give a reasonable explanation for non-attendance, the Sheriff may be ordered to withdraw from possession of the goods. An order for "no action" against the Sheriff may also be made. A costs order is likely to be made against the execution creditor to pay the Sheriff's costs and charges of the interpleader proceedings. He may also be ordered to pay the costs of the claimant.

If neither party attends the hearing then there is authority to allow the Court to make an order for the Sheriff to sell sufficient goods to pay for his costs and charges. He will then be withdrawn from possession and may seek an order for no action against him by either party (see *Eveleigh v. Salsbury* (1836) 5 Dowl 369).

Implementation of the Orders

The Sheriff's solicitor should check compliance with any order by setting review dates and informing the parties in writing. If orders are not complied with, a letter should be sent asking for a reason. If this proves unsatisfactory, the interpleader summons should be restored for a short appointment to bring the matter to the attention of the Master, who may make an "unless" type order. The execution creditor's solicitor's view should be sought before the summons is restored. Generally he or she will be willing to have a further hearing so that the matter can be moved along.

Usually the Sheriff's solicitor monitors the carrying out of the order and should help the parties wherever possible.

Stage 11 : Working Through Directions - Points to Note

Vigilance and proper reporting by the Sheriff's solicitor and Officer will help to ensure that walking possession can be maintained. Effective communication can help to ensure that the proceedings are dealt with as quickly as possible, so that a final order can be obtained.

Time Limits for Complying with Order

The Sheriff's solicitor should take the initiative in ensuring that the parties complete the directions according to any "interlocutory" orders. Sometimes the parties are unable to meet particular dates, but the Sheriff's solicitor should monitor what is happening and if concerned on any aspect of the proceedings, should restore the summons for further directions.

Safety of the Goods

A signed walking possession agreement is essential if walking possession is to be allowed throughout the proceedings. The name and status of the person signing the form should also be checked. If the goods are removed without the Sheriff's knowledge during the proceedings the Sheriff's solicitor should do the following:

(a) ask the Officer for as much information as possible about the circumstances of the removal;

(b) attend Court for an order that the goods be returned to the custody of the Sheriff forthwith and seek to have the order endorsed with a penal notice. Failure to comply with the order may lead to possible committal proceedings for contempt;

(c) send or fax a letter to the claimant or his solicitors, stating that the goods claimed by the claimant have been removed and asking the claimant if he has any information about that removal. It is also worth pointing out in the letter, that as the claimant has claimed these goods and presumably knows nothing about their removal, that the matter has been reported to the police. The name and address of the police station should also be requested.

Allowing Trading

The Officer may decide that the claimant/debtor should

be allowed to continue to trade after seizure. If that decision is made it is important that:

(a)   a full inventory is taken at once of the goods seized;

(b)   that a walking possession form is signed by the claimant;

(c)   that the execution creditor and Sheriff's solicitor are advised of the position, ie, that the claimant/debtor is being allowed to trade.

If either party is concerned about the position then an application should be made to the Court for directions.

Problems can arise. It may be the claimant will re-stock the premises with goods which are all subject to retention of title clauses (see above).

The position was considered in the case of *Re Dalton* (1963). In that case the Court took the view that the Sheriff - if deciding to allow trading - would have to return to the premises and make a fresh levy on all goods brought in in substitution of trading stock. This judgment would seem to imply that the Officer would have to keep a very accurate record of what was brought in. But there is still the need to guard against stock being subject to retention of title clauses.

The sensible course is for the Sheriff to write at once to the debtor or claimant or both if appropriate, saying that the goods are subject to the Sheriff's seizure, and that the Sheriff will allow trading to continue provided the level of stock is maintained with replacement stock that is not subject to retention of title clauses which will be available for the benefit of the execution creditor if the claimant's claim is subsequently barred.

Cars (see also ch.4)

Because of the cost of removal and storage of motor cars and their low auction value the decision to remove a car for sale is never easy. Some Officers will only seize a vehicle with the express instructions of the execution creditor. Before removing a car a DVLA search should be carried out.

The execution creditor can then be advised of the registered keeper and other details relating to the car. If the vehicle is to be seized then the execution creditor must again be warned of the possible removal and storage costs. If the execution creditor requests the car be seized but the Sheriff remains in walking possession then the Sheriff's Officer must return to make formal seizure of the vehicle and obtain a signed walking possession form in respect of it. At the same time the Sheriff's solicitor should write to the execution creditor pointing out that the Sheriff cannot be liable if the vehicle is moved, driven away or damaged and the Sheriff will not be responsible for the car's insurance. If any problems arise then an application must be made to the Court for directions.

It is possible however for the Sheriff's Officer to persuade the debtor/claimant to sign a walking possession agreement the wording of which will be that the vehicle will be returned to the custody of the Sheriff when required, that his insurers be notified of the Sheriff's interest in the vehicle and that he will agree to hand over the insurance proceeds if the vehicle is damaged beyond repair.

Possible Insolvency

The impact of insolvency on the execution is generally to

prevent the execution creditor having the benefit of the execution in preference to other creditors of the judgment debtor.

The Officer should be aware of insolvency procedures, such as Interim Orders, which do not require service of an order on the Sheriff. Generally these types of order find their way to the Sheriff's solicitor through the Officer and the contact he has with the judgment debtor or claimant. Again any information that the Officer receives about the possible insolvency of the judgment debtor should be immediately communicated to the Sheriff's solicitor who in turn should inform the parties of this possibility.

Stage 12 : The Final Hearing and Next Steps

Preparing for the Final Hearing

The Sheriff's solicitor should take the initiative in preparing for the Summary Disposal (or possible Trial of an Issue). The evidence in support of the claim should be placed in paginated bundles. The Sheriff's solicitor should co-ordinate the preparation of the bundles to assist the Court. Documents such as the writ of execution, interpleader summons, letter of claim, inventory and interlocutory orders should be included in the bundle. If available, photographs should be mounted and included. A simple chronology of events, similar to the information set out in Stage 5, should be placed at the beginning of the bundle. A bundle should be prepared for each party and for the use of the Court. Original affidavits need to be bespoken from Room E07 in the Central Office of the Royal Courts of Justice at least two clear days before the hearing (see RSC, O.63/4/2). District Registry practice should be checked.

Advocacy

Interpleader proceedings are the Sheriff's application to the Court for interpleader relief. Therefore at all times the Sheriff's solicitor has the conduct of the proceedings and should present the relevant facts to the Court. They should introduce themselves as solicitors for the Sheriff of the bailiwick in question and should then introduce the parties' representatives to the Court. A brief summary of events, using the chronology as a guide, should be given to the Master for the benefit of all parties present. Once this has been completed, the parties will present their evidence. The Sheriff's solicitor should assist the Court on questions of fact and law if required. Occasionally Officers will be asked to give evidence at these hearings and may be cross examined by the parties' solicitors.

The Final Order

After hearing all the evidence at a Summary Disposal hearing (or at the Trial of an Issue - see Stage 10 above) the Master or District Judge will make a final order to determine whether the claimant owns the goods which have been claimed.

The most frequent orders made are:

Interpleader Order No.1 (Queen's Bench Master's Practice Form No.28) which bars the claim, and
Interpleader Order No.1A (Queen's Bench Master's Practice Form No.29) where the claim is allowed.

The forms appear in the appendix to this chapter numbered 2 and 3 respectively.

Both orders provide for "no action" to be brought against the Sheriff provided the Sheriff has acted properly. The order will not be made if the claimant can show a "substantial grievance" against the Sheriff. In considering whether to make the order the Court will look at all the circumstances surrounding the execution of the warrant including the value of the goods and the claimant's conduct. Where a Sheriff sells goods subsequently found to belong to the claimant the Court can still make an order for "no action " against the Sheriff unless the claimant can set out an arguable case that the Sheriff had no defence to his actions either under statute or the common law (see *Observer Ltd v. Gordon* (1983) 2 All ER 945 and s.138B Supreme Court Act 1981, as inserted by the Statute Law (Repeals) Act 1989 sch.4 which repealed the Bankruptcy and Deeds of Arrangement Act 1913, s.15).

Informing the Officer

If an order is made barring the claim, then the Sheriff's solicitor should inform the Officer as soon as practicable. Ideally the Officer should attend to remove the goods the next working day after the hearing.

Occasionally, although a claim barred order is made, the execution creditor will give instructions for no action to be taken under the warrant, perhaps because he can negotiate an instalment arrangement with the judgment debtor. Both Sheriff's solicitor and Officer should consider carefully how to deal with the execution of the warrant in these circumstances and keep the matter under review.

Release of Claimed Goods

When a claim has been admitted, the Officer must withdraw from possession of those goods. If the goods are in storage he must make arrangements for the goods to be released. The goods should be released to the party from whom they were obtained (usually the debtor).

If it is necessary to allow the claimant to have the goods, for example if the debtor has vanished, the Officer should obtain a letter from the claimant indemnifying the Sheriff against any action which may be brought against him because of the delivery of the goods. That letter should also confirm that the goods have been returned in a sound condition.

As a matter of good practice, if any goods are handed back to a party in the proceedings, a list of the returned goods should be prepared and should be signed by the person receiving the goods. Any damage to the goods should be marked on the list. If goods are not in a good condition then they should be marked "as found".

Appeals

An application to appeal against a claim barred order is not a stay of execution. Therefore the claimant must apply for a stay of execution under RSC, O.47, r.1 and then lodge his appeal.

The appeal must be lodged within five days (RSC, O.58, r.1(3)) of the decision of a Master, Admiralty Registrar or District Judge of the Family Division. In the case of an appeal from a District Registrar the application must be lodged within seven days after the making of the order (RSC, O.58, r.3(2)).

If the claim barred order has been executed and the

goods have been moved, then the appeal will need to be dealt with as quickly as possible, to prevent escalating storage charges. Indeed a claimant may be persuaded to pay the outstanding amount to the Sheriff to be held pending the outcome of the appeal to prevent additional charges from being incurred. Care must also be taken over arrangements for an auction sale, to prevent unnecessary stopped sale fees being incurred.

Once again, close co-operation is needed between the Sheriff's solicitor and Officer to ensure the parties are made fully aware of the extent of the costs and charges being incurred.

Stage 13 : Payment of the Sheriff's Interpleader Costs and Charges

Sheriff's Interpleader Costs

These should not be confused with the Sheriff's charges which are dealt with below. The Sheriff's interpleader costs are those of the Sheriff's solicitors in handling the interpleader proceedings and will usually be based on a pre-determined hourly or fixed fee basis. Ultimately they can be the subject of "taxation" proceedings under RSC O.62 where the Court will certify whether they are reasonable. In the absence of any misconduct the Sheriff will be entitled to be paid his reasonable costs and charges incurred from the commencement of the proceedings to the final order (*Searle v. Matthews* (1883) 19 QBD 77). But if he has acted improperly in commencing or continuing the proceedings, or has taken unnecessary steps, then he may be disallowed his own costs and may even be ordered to pay the other party's costs resulting from his behaviour.

The Sheriff's neutrality between the parties will be an important factor if he is to be successful in his claim for costs (*Fredericks & Pelham Timber Building v. Wilkins (Read, Claimant (1971) supra*).

The primary responsibility for the payment of the Sheriff's costs and charges rests with the execution creditor. This area of interpleader proceedings can cause confusion and in some cases disbelief! It is for that reason that the Sheriff's solicitor and Officer should be aware of the issue of costs and keep the parties, particularly the execution creditor, fully informed on the question of costs. There is no rule requiring the Sheriff to do so, it is simply a matter of good commercial practice.

Therefore, even when an order is made barring the claimant's claim, it will be the execution creditor who initially has to foot the bill for the Sheriff's costs and charges of the proceedings (*Smith v. Darlow* (1884) 26 CHD 605). The usual order will entitle the execution creditor to seek a "remedy over" against the claimant for those costs and charges, but this procedure will involve further application to the Court and will be unpopular, particularly if the value of the goods is low.

Sheriffs' Charges

The Sheriff's charges are calculated according to the Sheriff's Fee Order which is dealt with in ch.16. Ultimately the reasonableness of the Sheriff's charges can be dealt with on taxation (*Long v. Bray, ex parte Wright* (1862) 10 WR 841). However, rather than waiting for taxation, a better practice would be for the Court to be asked to deal with the charges in the final order in the proceedings. Again, the Sheriff's solicitor can anticipate if a problem is going to arise, by understanding the breakdown of the charges before the final hearing.

Position if Served With Insolvency Notice

Sheriff's Interpleader Costs - the Sheriff will obtain a final order from the Court and the payment of the Sheriff's interpleader costs will be dependent on the terms of that order.

Sheriff's charges - the Sheriff will be entitled to payment of his charges up to the time of service of the insolvency notice (see *Re Harrison, ex parte Sheriff of Essex* (1893) 2 QB 111). The charges become a first charge upon the goods (see s.184(2) and s.346(2) Insolvency Act 1986) but poundage on goods handed over to the Trustee or Official Receiver is not chargeable (*Re Thomas, ex parte Sheriff of Middlesex* (1899) 1 QB 460 and see also ch.16.)

If possession money has increased due to some delay during the proceedings for which the Sheriff is not responsible then he is entitled to possession money for the entire period. However, if his possession was not proper then he will not be so entitled.

Appendix of Interpleader Forms

NOTICE OF CLAIM TO GOODS TAKEN IN EXECUTION
(Order 17, rule 2)

In the High Court of Justice
................................Division

Between   ....Plaintiff

and   ....Defendant

Take notice that _____(insert claimant)_____

has/have claimed certain goods taken in execution by the Sheriff
under warrant of execution issued in this action. You are hereby
required to admit or dispute the title of the said claimant to the said
goods and give notice thereof in writing to the said Sheriff within
seven days from the receipt of this notice, failing which the said
Sheriff may issue an interpleader summons. If you admit the title
of the said claimant to the said goods and give notice thereof in the
manner aforesaid to the said Sheriff you will only be liable for any
fees or expenses incurred prior to the receipt of the notice admitting
the claim.

Dated this   day of   19

To the Plaintiff and his Solicitors

_____

_____

                                    Officers to the Sheriff
                                    (see over for reply)

To (the Sheriffs Officers)
   (address)

NOTICE OF CLAIM TO GOODS TAKEN IN EXECUTION
(Order 17, rule 2)

In the High Court of Justice
...............................Division

Between   ....Plaintiff

and   ....Defendant

Take Notice that I admit/dispute the title of _____

(insert claimant) _____

to the goods seized by you under the execution issued under the judgment in this action.

Plaintiffs or Solicitors

Dated this   day of   19

FORM 1 INTERPLEADER SUMMONS

IN THE HIGH COURT OF JUSTICE
QUEEN'S BENCH DIVISION
       DISTRICT REGISTRY
MASTER   **Master in Chambers**
B E T W E E N :

                                               Plaintiff

           and

                                      Defendant
                                        Claimant

INTERPLEADER SUMMONS

LET ALL PARTIES concerned attend the Master in Chambers, Room No   , at the Central Office, Royal Courts of Justice, Strand, London WC2A 2LL, on   the   day of 199   at   o'clock in the   noon, on the hearing of an application on the part of the Sheriff of   that the execution creditor and the claimant appear and state the nature and particulars of their respective claims to the goods and chattels seized, or intended to be seized by the above-named sheriff under the writ of fieri facias issued in this action and maintain or relinquish the same, and abide by such order as may be made herein, and that in the meantime, all further proceedings be stayed.

To the Claimant: take notice that within 14 days of service of this summons you are required to make an affidavit specifying any money and describing any goods and chattels claimed and setting out the grounds upon which such claim is based and do serve copies of such affidavit upon the execution creditor and the sheriff.

DATED the   day of   19
This Summons was taken out by
Solicitors for the Applicant

    To: Solicitors for the above-named Execution Creditor

And to:
    the above-named Claimant

FORM 2 : INTERPLEADER ORDER NO.1

IN THE HIGH COURT OF JUSTICE
QUEEN'S BENCH DIVISION
      DISTRICT REGISTRY
MASTER   **Master in Chambers**
B E T W E E N :

                                        Plaintiff

           and

                                    Defendant

                                    Claimant

INTERPLEADER ORDER NO.1

UPON HEARING the Solicitor for the Execution Creditor and the Solicitor for the Sheriff of

IT IS ORDERED that:
1   the Claimant be barred and that no action be brought against the above named Sheriff
2   the Claimant do pay to the Execution Creditor the costs of the Interpleader proceedings including the costs of the application to be taxed, and that the Execution Creditor do pay to the Sheriff his costs and charges of the interpleader proceedings, including the application, and his possession money caused by the claim of the Claimant to be taxed with remedy over against the Claimant

Dated

FORM 3 : INTERPLEADER ORDER NO.1A

IN THE HIGH COURT OF JUSTICE
QUEEN'S BENCH DIVISION
          DISTRICT REGISTRY
MASTER   **Master in Chambers**
B E T W E E N :

                                                      Plaintiff

                              and

                                                      Defendant
                                                      Claimant

_____

INTERPLEADER ORDER NO.1A

_____

UPON HEARING the Solicitor for the Execution Creditor, the Solicitor for the Claimant and the Solicitor for the Sheriff of

IT IS ORDERED that:
1   the said Sheriff do withdraw from possession of the goods seized by him under the Writ of *Fieri Facias* herein
2   no action be brought against the said Sheriff
3   the Execution Creditor do pay to the Sheriff his costs and charges of the Interpleader Proceedings herein to be taxed

Dated

FORM 4 : DIRECTIONS ORDER

IN THE HIGH COURT OF JUSTICE
QUEEN'S BENCH DIVISION
          DISTRICT REGISTRY
MASTER   Master in Chambers
B E T W E E N :

                                                            Plaintiff
                              and

                                                            Defendant
                                                            Claimant

---

INTERLOCUTORY ORDER FOR DIRECTIONS

UPON HEARING the Solicitor for the Execution Creditor, the Solicitor for the Claimant and the Solicitor for the Sheriff of

IT IS ORDERED that:

1   Within 14 days from the date of this Order the said Claimant do make and serve upon the said Execution Creditor and Sheriff an Affidavit specifying any money and describing any goods and chattels claimed and setting out the grounds upon which such claim is based

2   Within 14 days of the date of this Order the said Claimant do make and serve upon the said Execution Creditor a List of Documents setting out all the documents which are or have been in his/her possession custody or power relating to the matters in issue in the Interpleader proceedings herein AND THAT there be inspection of those documents within 7 days thereafter

3   This Summons be adjourned to a private room appointment for Summary Disposal on a date to be fixed

4   Liberty to Restore

5   Costs reserved

Dated

CHAPTER 7

Insolvency

The passing into law of the Insolvency Acts of 1985 and 1986 simplified some aspects of insolvency law but inevitably introduced fresh and original problems for the Sheriff's Officer.

No longer could an individual debtor commit one of a number of acts of bankruptcy, no longer could seizure and sale by the Sheriff, or keeping house by the debtor be a basis for a bankruptcy petition. The principal requirement for a creditor to be able to petition for the bankruptcy of an individual or for the winding-up of a company, is to demonstrate either a lack of ability or an unwillingness to pay a debt. Where an attempt to execute a writ of *fi:fa* proves unsuccessful, the Sheriff can be requested to file a return stating "the execution was unsuccessful in part or in the whole". Such a return can then be used to support the petition (Insolvency Act, 1986, s.123 & s.268 and see also ch.10, Abortive Executions).

The 1986 Act gave greater emphasis to intermediate stages of insolvency, those of Voluntary Administration Orders, Interim Orders and other voluntary arrangements, and it is in dealing with these that fresh difficulties have arisen.

In dealing with insolvencies, it is essential that the form of insolvency be identified and that the responsibilities of those acting be understood. A list of definitions and descriptions is given at the end of this chapter.

The Act (s.388 *et seq*) imposes restrictions as to the qualifications of persons permitted to act as Insolvency Practitioners and the Officer should expect to be dealing with experienced and professional advisers, liquidators and trustees.

The execution creditor is entitled to proceed by means of an execution warrant until there is a successful petition for a bankruptcy order, a winding-up order of a company or a voluntary order. Whether the creditor may retain the benefit of the execution will depend on the progress of the warrant and the timing of the petitions. Voluntary arrangements may take effect as an interim stay of execution, leaving both creditor and Sheriff in a state of limbo by preventing progress on a warrant while not necessarily denying the creditor the benefits already received.

Voluntary Arrangements - Individuals

Application may be made to the court for an Interim Order. This is similar to an application for an Administration Order. It is intended to allow a debtor and his advisers an opportunity to rescue an insolvent situation, and to enter into a scheme of arrangement with the creditors. The making of an Interim Order stops all execution being continued or commenced without the leave of the Court, (*ibid.*, s.252).

The mere application for an Interim Order is not a stay of execution, but the Court may stay any action, execution or legal process pending the order. The practice followed since the commencement of the Act appears to be such that a stay is granted whenever the application is lodged (*ibid.*, s.254).

Unlike the case of company insolvency, there is no requirement for the Sheriff to be served with notice of either the application or the order, and so the Officer may find that he has proceeded in breach of a "stay". Problems have arisen where the Sheriff is in possession of goods and where monies have been paid under the execution.

We suggest that Sheriff's charges in such cases should fall within the ambit of the Insolvency Rules 5.28 (which is similar to Rule.1.28 referring to companies).

The Interim Order ceases to have effect after 14 days but the Court may extend the order on application by the Nominee Supervisor - who is the insolvency practitioner advising the debtor, (*ibid.*, s.255, s.256).

Monies held by the Sheriff

Whilst the Insolvency Act, 1986, is unclear as to the rights of the supervisor, a decision was made in Burnley County Court by Mr Registrar R.H. Haythornthwaite on November 3, 1988 in the matter of *Ian Doney*. The Sheriff had levied and had received five payments, but was prevented from proceeding further by the making of an Interim Order. The supervisor sought to claim the monies. He acknowledged he would not have claimed monies received directly by the creditor, he was only seeking monies held by the Sheriff.

The Registrar said "To sum up, I have no doubt whatever the supervisor's claim to the monies held by the Sheriff fails. The monies belong to the execution creditor and should be paid to him forthwith."

Goods Held by the Sheriff

A different situation arose over the surrender of goods by

the Sheriff to a supervisor. The Sheriff had levied at shop premises but could not proceed in view of an Interim Order. Mr Registrar Ashworth of Blackburn County Court held, in the matter of *Peake* on July 15, 1987, that the goods already seized are liable to be returned to the supervisor of the arrangement for disposal by him for the general benefit of the creditors.

Secured Creditor

In the matter of *Julian Hannaville Ackroyd Peck v. Raymond Craighead and Others* before Mr Martin Mann, QC, sitting as a Deputy Judge of the Chancery Division on January 18, 1995, (*Times Law Report*, February 1995) it was held that where a creditor has issued execution to the Sheriff and where the Sheriff is in walking possession of the goods of the debtor, the execution creditor is in the position of a secured creditor for the purposes of s.258(4) of the Insolvency Act 1986. In reaching this conclusion the Judge followed the dicta of Lindley MR, in *re Charles Clark* 1988 1 Ch 336 at p.339.

Thus, where Individual Voluntary Arrangements are approved under s.252 of the Act, and the secured creditor does not assent to the arrangements proposed at the meeting of creditors held under s.257, such arrangements may be upset by the creditor under the provisions of s.262.

The Sheriff should not proceed to sell in the face of a voluntary arrangement in these circumstances unless the execution creditor obtains an order under s.262 allowing him to do so.

Administration Order - County Court

There is a distinction between an Administration Order or an Interim Order made under s.11 or s.252 of the Insolvency Act and an Administration Order made under Part V1.6 of the County Court Act 1984 (ss.112 to 117).

When an Administration Order is made under s.114, County Court Act 1984, no creditor shall have any remedy against the property of the debtor, but only in respect of debts notified to the Court before the Administration Order was made or in respect of those which have subsequently become scheduled to the order by addition to the list of debts.

It would be prudent for the Sheriff, if he learns of such an Administration Order, to confirm with the execution creditor that the debt is not "a scheduled debt" and therefore not bound by the order. The debtor may apply to the Court to have further debts scheduled, indeed the County Court Act clearly contemplates the later addition of unscheduled debts.

BANKRUPTCY

Although the procedures regarding the insolvency of individuals are broadly similar to those relating to companies, they differ in certain aspects as they are designed to deal with different problems.

Beyond the Interim Order referred to earlier, there is no equivalent in Bankruptcy to the Voluntary Liquidation of a company. A Bankruptcy Order is an order of the Court designed to protect a debtor from the pressures of his insolvency and to ensure that his assets are equitably distributed amongst his creditors. The Official Receiver or a Trustee is appointed and has control of the bankrupt's affairs. The bankrupt is obliged to surrender his assets to the Trustee and to declare all details of his debts and commitments.

As in liquidation, the Officer must pay particular attention to the dates of events, dates of payments and so on, so that he may deal properly with any proceeds of the execution, goods or monies received. The pattern and importance of these dates may differ from the requirements in liquidation.

Bankruptcy - Petitions

A creditor may petition for the bankruptcy of a debtor on the grounds that the debtor has failed to acknowledge a statutory demand for payment, or on the grounds that "execution or other process issued in respect of the debt on a judgment or other order of any court in favour of the petitioning creditor .... has been returned unsatisfied in whole or in part." (Insolvency Act, 1986, s.268).

A debtor may present his own petition on the grounds that he is unable to pay his debts, and an order may also be made in criminal bankruptcy. (*Ibid.*, ss.272, 277).

Bankruptcy - Commencement

Until the new Act, bankruptcy commenced at the commission of an act of bankruptcy or at the date the petition was presented. However, the 1986 Act changed this; commencement is now the date on which a Bankruptcy Order is made and not the date of the presentation of the petition. This is particularly relevant when considering the right of a Trustee to recover monies from creditors. The Trustee no longer has the right to set aside transactions which may have taken place after the commission of one of the old acts of bankruptcy but he may seek to recover monies paid directly to a judgment creditor under an incomplete execution on the grounds that such monies were not paid to, and held by, the Sheriff for 14 days, (*ibid.*, ss.278, 346; *re Godding* (1914) 2 KB 70; *re Pollock* (1902) 87 LT 238).

Bankruptcy - Restriction on Proceedings

Where a petition has been presented, the Court may stay action under an existing judgment. After the making of the Order, no creditor who has a debt provable in the bankruptcy may commence an action without the consent of the court (*ibid.*, s.285).

Bankruptcy - Effect on the Sheriff

The creditor is not entitled to retain the benefit of an execution which has not been completed at the commencement of the bankruptcy. In addition, any monies held by the Sheriff under a judgment issued for £500 or over (Insolvency Proceedings (Monetary Limits) Order 1986, No.1996), may be claimed by the Trustee if those funds have not been held by the Sheriff for a period of 14 days. The Sheriff's charges, applicable to monies and goods surrendered to the Trustee, are a first charge on those monies or goods.

Monies Held

The Sheriff must hold monies for 14 days before

accounting to the creditor. If within that period he is served with notice of a bankruptcy petition or of a bankruptcy order, he must continue to hold the monies until they are claimed by the Trustee (*ibid.*, s.346).

The 14 Day Period

The note in RSC at O.3/2/2, General Rules of Computation of Time, gives as such a general rule:

> "that where a period of time or after a given date is prescribed as the period in which an act is to be done, the day of that date or event is to be excluded in the computation of the period, and the act is to be done on or before the last day of the period."

Effectively, this means the monies become "free" and should be paid over on the 15th day. For example, monies received on February 9 would not become "free" until the close of business on February 23, and could thus be paid away first thing on the 24th.

In the event of a sale being held under an execution, the 14 days run from the date of the sale, not the date of receipt of the monies. (s.346 and see also *Cripps Ross & Co, ex parte Ross* (1888) 21 QBD, at p.472). Therefore, payment could be made on the 15th day after the day of the sale.

Service of Documents

The Insolvency Rules (SI 1986 No.1925) r.12.19(2) states:

> "... the notice shall be in writing and be delivered by

hand at, or sent by recorded delivery to, the office of the under-sheriff or (as the case may be) of the officer charged with the execution."

Service of documents such as notices of petitions, meetings of creditors, liquidator's request to deliver, etc, should be on the Sheriff at the address of the Under Sheriff and not on the Officer (*Hellyer v. Sheriff of Yorkshire* (1974) 2 All ER 712).

The Act, s.184 states:

"In this section ... the Sheriff includes any officer charged with the execution of a writ or other process."

This phrase was also contained in the Companies Act, 1948, s.326 which was the legislation in force when *Hellyer* was decided. The Officer is not obliged to assist companies and insolvency practitioners in their duties but if notice is served upon the Officer, it does no harm to invite the parties to effect proper service. The relevant date of service is when the Under Sheriff receives the documents.

Service by Fax Transmission

Documents may only be served by fax transmission where the method of service is not prescribed by statute. Therefore, notice of insolvency cannot be by fax transmission as the strict requirement is for service to be by hand or by recorded delivery at the office of the Under Sheriff (*Hastie and Jenkerson v. McMahon* (1990) CA. *The Times*, April 3).

Goods Held and Surrendered

The Trustee may require the Sheriff to surrender goods seized but not yet sold. When the Officer is made aware of the making of a Bankruptcy Order and the Sheriff has been served correctly, he should arrange for the Trustee to take over the goods. The charges incurred are payable by the Trustee who has authority to sell sufficient to satisfy the costs, (*ibid.*, s.346).

The Officer should exercise caution; it is not unknown for a Trustee to accept a third party claim, submitted at some time later, and to decline to pay the Sheriff's costs on the grounds that no "goods of the debtor" have been surrendered. This may come to light after a prolonged delay, a delay which may affect the Officer's ability to recover the costs from the execution creditor.

The question of delivery of goods to the Trustee or Liquidator and the subsequent ability of the trustee/liquidator to deal with those goods was referred to in the case of *Wells, ex parte Sheriff of Kent* (1893) 68 LT 231. The Trustee had been unable to sell the goods as the landlord had distrained. It appears that the Sheriff is entitled to his fees, even if the trustee/liquidator cannot sell the goods, provided there has been "physical delivery" of the goods by the Sheriff to the trustee/liquidator. Delivery is a positive step, an event which actually takes place.

A practical procedure is for the Officer to submit, in the first instance, an account of charges to both the Trustee and the creditor, repaying the creditor if and when the Trustee accounts.

Lack of Request to Deliver

Where no request is served, the duty to proceed and sell

remains unaltered by the Bankruptcy Order, except that the monies are not paid to the creditor. Lord Esher, MR, said:

> "I think that, if no request is made, his (the Sheriff's) duty to sell remains unaltered and unaffected by the receiving order. He must proceed with the execution and sell the goods; but, when he has done so, the creditor is not to have the benefit, but the proceeds must be handed to the receiver or trustee less the expenses to which the Sheriff is entitled." (*Woolford's Estate v. Levy* (1892) 66 LT 812).

The Insolvency Act, 1986 does not impose an automatic stay when, unlike a Winding-up Order, a Bankruptcy Order is made. The onus is upon the Trustee to take the positive step of calling upon the Sheriff to deliver the goods to him.

Creditor's Rights

The rights of the Trustee may, upon application, be set aside by the Court in favour of the creditor (*ibid.*, s.346(6)).

After Acquired Property and Debts

A creditor may not commence proceedings in respect of a debt provable in the bankruptcy (s.346(1)) but s.346(8) suggests that after-acquired property may be available for seizure unless the Trustee has served notice that he claims it as part of the estate. This would appear to imply that a creditor may sue and proceed in respect of a debt not covered by the bankruptcy, provided always that the execution is restricted to the "after-acquired" property not claimed by the Trustee.

Liquidation of a Partnership

The Insolvent Partnerships Order 1986 states in Part 2, s.7:

> "The provisions of Part V of the Act specified in Schedule 1 to this Order shall apply to the winding-up of insolvent partnerships as unregistered companies with the modifications specified in that Schedule where no insolvency petition is presented by the petitioner against an insolvent member."

Part 5 of the Insolvency Act 1986 relates to the winding-up of unregistered companies and, at s.220, defines these as:

> "... the expression 'unregistered company' includes any trustee savings bank certified under the enactments relating to such banks, any association and any company, with the following exceptions -
>
> (a) a railway company incorporated by Act of Parliament,
> (b) a company registered in any part of the United Kingdom under the Joint Stock Companies or under legislation (past or present) relating to companies in Great Britain."

(The reference to trustee savings banks has since been repealed).

In Part 3, s.8 it states:

"(1) ss. 220(1) and 221 of the Act shall apply to the winding-up of insolvent partnerships as unregistered companies where an insolvency petition is presented by the petitioner against two or more insolvent members with the following modifications:

(a)   in s.220(1) before the words 'any association' there shall be inserted the words 'any insolvent partnership';

(b)   deals with the application of the act to insolvent partnerships whose principal place of business is in England and Wales;

(c)   for s.221(5) there shall be substituted the following -

(5) the circumstances in which an insolvent partnership may be wound up are that the partnership is unable to pay its debts."

Section 228, Insolvency Act 1986 states:

"Where an order has been made for the winding-up of an unregistered company, no action shall be proceeded with or commenced against any contributory of the company in respect of any debt of the company, except by leave of the court, and subject to such terms as the court may impose."

These sections imply a distinction between partnership debts and personal debts, they are primarily concerned with the former. However, s.227 extends the power of the Court to stay proceedings against a contributory prior to the making of a winding-up order. Unregistered companies (including partnerships) may only be wound up when a petition is presented, they may not be wound up voluntarily (s.221(4)).

Voluntary Arrangements - Companies

Application may be made to the Court for an Administration Order, which is effectively a procedure whereby an Insolvency Practitioner reports to the Court as to the possibility of rescuing an insolvent situation rather than immediate liquidation. If the Court approves the scheme, an Administrator will be appointed who will have conduct of the insolvent company's affairs. An application for such an order acts as a stay of execution and any creditor is barred from commencing proceedings and from continuing with an execution. It must be stressed that this "stay" is effective from the time of the application, not from the making of the order. As soon as the Officer is aware of the application, he must cease all process, must not remove goods, must not proceed to a sale of goods already removed, but must merely await the outcome of the application. (Insolvency Act, 1986, s.10 (1) (c)).

The petitioner is required to serve notice of the petition on "any sheriff or other officer who to his knowledge is charged with an execution or other legal process against the company or its property ....." (Insolvency (Amendment) Rules, (SI 1987 No.1919) introducing Rule 2.6A).

An application for an Administration Order may prove to have a detrimental effect on the creditor's situation in terms of accruing costs, particularly if the application is adjourned. For that reason, at the earliest opportunity, all parties involved should be made aware of any action taken under a warrant.

The Act does not place a specific obligation upon the Administrator to pay the Sheriff's charges on taking over the goods when the order is made. The Insolvency Rules do refer to costs and charges being payable where those costs would have been payable had the order been made in bankruptcy or liquidation, and it may be argued that these sections extend to the Sheriff's charges, (Insolvency Rules, 1986, (SI 1986 No.1925) Rule 1.28).

Once the Administration Order is made, any outstanding winding-up petition shall be dismissed, any administrative receiver shall vacate office and all creditors are barred from commencing or continuing with legal process or distraint, unless the consent of the administrator is given. The Sheriff must therefore withdraw, (Insolvency Act, 1986, s.11).

COMPANIES - LIQUIDATION

As a company is a legal entity in its own right, procedures have to be followed to terminate its existence - the liquidation of the company. Liquidation entails the cessation of business and the appointment of an insolvency practitioner to oversee the collection of debts and the realization of the assets. Most aspects of liquidation do not concern the Officer, the exceptions being his duties on commencement of liquidation, the surrender of assets seized and monies recovered, and to obtain settlement of the Sheriff's charges where they are payable by the liquidator. In order that he may appreciate his duties and comply with the legislation and rules, the Officer must be aware of the difference between Voluntary and Compulsory Liquidation. The first is the process whereby liquidation occurs at the instigation of the members of the company and with the consent of the creditors, the second is where the liquidation is the subject of a Court order, normally at the instigation of a disappointed creditor.

It is important to pay heed to the dates on which events occur, for upon these dates much depends; the voidability of a writ of *fi:fa*, the beneficiary of the proceeds of the writ and so on.

Action to be taken

Where the Officer is in possession of goods and is aware of a resolution for the winding-up, or the presentation of a petition seeking a winding-up order, he should immediately advise the creditor's solicitors and should contact the proposed liquidator if he has been identified. It must, however, be remembered that the proposed liquidator will have no authority to act until he has been formally appointed. It is not unusual to find that some insolvency practitioners assume authority and seek to instruct the Sheriff or interfere with the assets when they are only in an advisory position.

During 1994 the Sheriff of Kent was in possession under a writ of *fi:fa*. Liquidation of the debtor company was proposed and insolvency practitioners appointed to convene the appropriate meetings. The insolvency practitioners removed the goods without the consent of the Sheriff and refused to return the goods despite still not having convened the meeting of creditors. A writ was issued upon the partners of the accountants involved for "the return of the goods detained by them ... or their value ... and damages for their detention together with interest ...". Service of the writ had an immediate effect, the goods were returned to the Sheriff and the costs of the proceedings were paid by the insolvency practitioners.

On a practical basis, co-operation may prove to be in the best interests of all concerned, but the Officer must never fail to be conscious of his duty to the creditor who instructs him. Similarly he should remember that a proposed liquidator may not necessarily be appointed.

Rights of the Creditor

Commencement of liquidation will deny the creditor the benefit of the execution but he may apply to have the rights of the liquidator set aside in his (the creditor's) favour (Insolvency Act, 1986, s.184).

For these reasons, it may be practical and prudent to delay removal and sale (provided always that the assets are secure), but it may be equally practical not to abandon procedures already commenced, for example, a sale already arranged. The circumstances of each case must be examined and considered, the costs involved in each evaluated and, where possible, action taken in the best interests of the judgment creditor.

Voluntary Liquidation - Commencement, Effect, etc

A company may be wound up voluntarily; the commencement is the date on which the resolution is passed, (*ibid.*, s.86), and notice must be given in the Gazette within 14 days from the passing of the resolution, (s.85). However, "if a creditor has had notice of a meeting having been called at which a resolution for voluntary winding-up is to be proposed, the date on which he had notice is substituted for the purpose of subs.(1) for the date of commencement of the winding up." (s.183).

Section 183(1) states that a creditor may not retain the

benefit of an execution which was not completed prior to the commencement of winding-up.

If the directors are able to make a Statutory Declaration of Solvency as defined in s.89, the liquidation will be "Members' Voluntary". If the directors are unable to make that declaration, the liquidation will be "Creditors' Voluntary", (*ibid.,* s.90).

If, on the day of the creditors' meeting, the directors have not made the Statutory Declaration of Solvency or where the members' liquidator is of the opinion that the company will be unable to pay its debts within the period stated in the declaration, the winding-up becomes Creditors' Voluntary, (*ibid.,* s.95,96).

The creditors and members shall nominate a liquidator; if the nominees differ, that chosen by the creditors shall take office, but the members may apply to the court to have their nominee appointed jointly, (s.100).

Compulsory Liquidation

A company may be wound up by the Court for several reasons, (s.122), including inability to pay its debts; the definition of "unable to pay its debts" includes "if in England and Wales, execution or other process issued on a judgment, decree or order of any court in favour of a creditor is returned unsatisfied in whole or in part" (*ibid.,* s.123).

The company or any creditor or contributory of the company may apply to the Court to have all proceedings, executions, etc, stayed where a winding-up petition has been presented but not yet granted (*ibid.,* s.126).

Compulsory - Commencement and Validity of Writ

The commencement, in the case of compulsory liquidation, is the date on which the petition was presented, or the date of the passing of a resolution to wind-up, if that took place earlier (*ibid.*, s.129). This is of importance when considering the validity of a writ, as any levy or distress put into force after the commencement of compulsory liquidation is void. Any action taken can be ignored by the Liquidator and the costs fall upon the creditor (*ibid.*, s.128).

Compulsory - Effect of the Order

Once a winding-up order has been made, no action or proceeding may be commenced or continued without the leave of the Court (*ibid.*, s.130). Thus, any action continued under a warrant may be set aside, although the Liquidator may not have served the Sheriff with notice under s.184. The Officer should not withdraw but must not proceed further. He should immediately contact the Liquidator and advise him of the current position of the writ.

Liquidators - General

The Liquidator is appointed to deal with the assets of the company and to discharge the debts according to the priorities established by statute. His obligation to deal with the Sheriff is stated in s.184, but it is interesting to note that in s.166 the members' Liquidator is not permitted to dispose of assets other than perishables if a creditors' meeting is being convened. He is, however, permitted to take control of the assets and take appropriate action for the protection of the assets.

The Court may appoint a Provisional Liquidator before the making of a winding-up order and his powers will be defined by the Court appointing him, (*ibid.,* s.135).

Liquidation and the Sheriff

"Where a creditor has issued execution against the goods or land of a company ... and the company is subsequently wound up, he is not entitled to retain the benefit of the execution ... against the liquidator unless he has completed the execution ... before the commencement of the winding up" (*ibid.,* s.183).

The Liquidator may request the Sheriff to deliver the goods and any money seized or received in part satisfaction of the execution to the Liquidator, but the costs of the execution become a first charge on the goods or money so delivered. By s.184(2) the Liquidator may sell sufficient of the goods to discharge these costs.

The Sheriff must hold all monies received under a judgment in excess of £500, (specified in Insolvency Proceedings (Monetary Limits) SI 1986 No.1996 but that sum may be altered by future order under the Act, s.416), for a period of 14 days before accounting to the creditor. If, within that time, notice is served that a winding-up petition has been presented, or a meeting of creditors convened for the purpose of appointing a Liquidator, or that a resolution has been passed commencing liquidation, the monies must be retained to the order of the Liquidator, (*ibid.,* s.184(3 & 4)).

Instalments or Piecemeal Payments

It has been long established that each and every payment made to the Sheriff to avoid a sale should have its own 14 day period (*in re Walkden Sheet Metal Co. Ltd* (1959) 3 All ER 333). It is necessary to review the entire history of the execution to ascertain which monies are due to the creditor and which to the Liquidator. In equity, costs should be apportioned in the same way.

Service on the Sheriff

Service of documents such as notices of petitions, meetings of creditors, liquidator's request to deliver, etc., should be on the Sheriff, by hand or by recorded delivery, at the address of the Under Sheriff and not on the Officer (*Hellyer v. Sheriff of Yorkshire* (1974) 2 All ER 712; Insolvency Rules (SI 1986 No.1925) rule 12.19(2)). This was discussed in detail earlier under Bankruptcy.

The Officer is not obliged to assist companies and insolvency practitioners in their duties but if notice is served upon the Officer, it does no harm to invite the parties to effect proper service. The relevant date of service is when the Under Sheriff receives the documents.

Service may not be effected by fax transmission as the method of service is prescribed otherwise, it must be by hand or by recorded delivery.

Should the Sheriff be served with notice of the presentation of a winding-up petition but the company is placed into voluntary liquidation instead, the notice of the petition does not bind monies in the hands of the Sheriff. The operative date is the serving of notice on the Sheriff of the convening of the meeting or of the passing of the resolution. The reverse is also true, where voluntary liquidation is commenced but compulsory liquidation intervenes (*Bluston Bramley Ltd v. Leigh* (1950) 2 All ER 30).

Company Struck Off

Execution cannot proceed against a company which has been struck off as it is no longer in existence. The effects of that company are classified as *bona vacantia*, (s.652, Companies Act 1985). However, relief is given to the creditor under s.653. Effectively the company may be "revived" and execution issued.

NOTES

Administrative Receiver. An insolvency practitioner who is appointed by a debenture holder over a company's property (either in part or in whole). His duty is to sell sufficient of the assets to repay the secured debts.

Administrator. An insolvency practitioner appointed by the court under an Administration Order to prepare a rescue plan. If the creditors consent, the plan would be implemented.

Bankruptcy. Personal insolvency following an order of the court.

Compulsory Liquidation. Winding-up of a company after a petition to the court.

Creditors' Voluntary Liquidation. The voluntary winding-up of an insolvent company (that is without a court order).

Fixed Charge. Security for a loan, secured on specified assets. In the event of default, the creditor may appoint a Receiver.

Floating Charge. Security for a loan, secured on the assets and business of a company without attaching to specific assets. In the event of default, the creditor may appoint an Administrative Receiver.

Insolvency Practitioner. An individual licensed by one of the approved bodies, eg. The Law Society, Institute of Insolvency Practitioners, Department of Trade etc.

Liquidator. Insolvency Practitioner appointed to wind up a company.

Members' Voluntary Liquidation. The winding-up of a solvent company where all the creditors will be paid in full.

Nominee. Insolvency Practitioner appointed to consider proposals under a voluntary arrangement.

Official Receiver. Member of the Department of Trade and an officer of the court who deals with bankruptcies and compulsory liquidations.

Receiver. Person appointed under a fixed charge to receive income from the secured and specified assets or to sell those assets.

Secured Creditor. Creditor who has a legal security over a debtor's assets.

Statutory Demand. Legal demand for payment within 21 days. In the event of default, a petition may be presented for the bankruptcy or compulsory liquidation of the debtor.

Supervisor. Insolvency Practitioner appointed to carry out a voluntary arrangement.

Trustee. Insolvency Practitioner appointed to deal with the estate of a bankrupt.

Voluntary Arrangement. Procedure which permits a debtor (company or individual) to make arrangements with their creditors to either pay the debts or reach agreement as to a compromise.

Winding-up Order. Order of the court for the winding-up of a company.

Principal Applicable Sections of the Insolvency Act 1986

Section 10 (1)
During the period beginning with the presentation of a petition for an administration order and ending with the making of such an order or the dismissal of the petition -

    (c) no other proceedings and no execution or other legal process may be commenced or continued, and no distress may be levied, against the company or its property except with the leave of the court and subject to such terms as aforesaid.

Section 11 (3)
During the period for which an administration order is in force -

    (d) no other proceedings and no execution or other legal process may be commenced or continued, and no distress may be levied, against the company or its property except with the consent of the administrator or the leave of the court and subject (where the court gives leave) to such terms as aforesaid.

Section 86
A voluntary winding up is deemed to commence at the time of the passing of the resolution for voluntary winding up.

Section 90

A winding up in the case of which a directors' statutory declaration under section 89 has been made is a "members' voluntary winding up": and a winding up in the case of which such a declaration has not been made is a "creditors' winding up".

Section 123

(1) A company is deemed unable to pay its debts -

   (a) if a creditor (by assignment or otherwise) to whom the company is indebted in a sum exceeding £750 then due has served on the company, by leaving it at the company's registered office, a written demand (in the prescribed form) requiring the company to pay the sum so due and the company has for three weeks thereafter neglected to pay the sum or to secure or compound for it to the reasonable satisfaction of the creditor, or

   (b) if, in England and Wales, execution or other process issued on a judgment, decree or order of any court in favour of a creditor of the company is returned unsatisfied in whole or in part, or

   (c) and (d) (deal with Scotland and Northern Ireland) or

   (e) if it is proved to the satisfaction of the court that the company is unable to pay its debts as they fall due.

Section 126

(1) At any time after the presentation of a winding-up petition, and before a winding-up order has been made, the company, or any creditor or contributory, may -

   (a) where any action or proceeding against the company is pending in the High Court or Court of Appeal in England and Wales or Northern Ireland, apply to the court in which the action or proceeding is pending for a stay of proceedings therein, and

(b)   where any other action or proceeding is pending against the company, apply to the court having jurisdiction to wind up the company to restrain further proceedings in the action or proceeding;

and the court to which application is so made may (as the case may be) stay, sist or restrain the proceedings accordingly on such terms as it thinks fit.

Section 128

(1)   Where a company registered in England and Wales is being wound up by the court, any attachment, sequestration, distress or execution put in force against the estate or effects of the company after the commencement of the winding-up is void.

(2)   This section, so far as relates to any estate or effects of the company situated in England and Wales, applies in the case of a company registered in Scotland as it applies in the case of a company registered in England and Wales.

Section 129

(1)   If, before the presentation of a petition for the winding-up of a company by the court, a resolution has been passed by the company for voluntary winding-up, the winding-up of the company is deemed to have commenced at the time of the passing of the resolution; and unless the court, on proof of fraud or mistake, directs otherwise, all proceedings taken in the voluntary winding-up are deemed to have been validly taken.

(2)   In any other case, the winding-up of a company by the court is deemed to commence at the time of the presentation of the petition for the winding-up.

Section 130

(2)   When a winding-up order has been made or a provisional liquidator has been appointed, no action or proceeding shall be proceeded with or commenced against the company or its property, except by leave of the court and subject to such terms as the court may impose.

Section 135

(1)   Subject to the provisions of this section, the court may, at any time after the presentation of a winding-up petition, appoint a liquidator provisionally.

(2)   In England and Wales, the appointment of a provisional liquidator may be made at any time before the making of a winding-up order; and either the official receiver or any other fit person may be appointed.

(3)   (deals with Scotland)

(4)   The provisional liquidator shall carry out such functions as the court may confer on him.

(5)   When a liquidator is provisionally appointed by the court, his powers may be limited by the order appointing him.

Section 183

(1)   Where a creditor has issued execution against the goods or land of a company or has attached any debt due to it, and the company is subsequently wound up, he is not entitled to retain the benefit of the execution or attachment against the liquidator unless he has completed the execution or attachment before the commencement of the winding up.

(2)   However,

   (a)   if the creditor has had notice of a meeting having been called at which a resolution for voluntary winding up is proposed, the date on which he had notice is substituted, for the purpose of subs.(1), for the date of commencement of the winding up;

   (b)   a person who purchases in good faith under a sale

by the sheriff any goods of the company on which
execution has been levied in all cases acquires a
good title to them against the liquidator; and

(c)   the rights conferred by subs.(1) on the liquidator
may be set aside by the court in favour of the
creditor to such an extent and subject to such terms
as the court thinks fit.

(3)   For the purposes of this Act -

(a)   an execution against goods is completed by seizure
and sale, or by the making of a charging order
under s.1 of the Charging Orders Act 1979.

(b)   an attachment of a debt is completed by receipt of
the debt; and

(c)   an execution against land is completed by seizure,
by the appointment of a receiver, or by the making
of a charging order under s.1 of the Act
above-mentioned.

(4)   In this section, "goods" includes all chattels personal and
"the sheriff" includes any officer charged with the
execution of a writ or other process.

Section 184

(1)   The following applies where a company's goods are taken
in execution and, before their sale or the completion of
the execution (by the receipt or recovery of the full
amount of the levy), notice is served on the sheriff that
a provisional liquidator has been appointed or that a
winding-up order has been made, or that a resolution for
voluntary winding-up has been passed.

(2)   The sheriff shall, on being so required, deliver the goods
and any money seized or received in part satisfaction of
the execution to the liquidator; but the costs of execution
are a first charge on the goods or money so delivered, and
the liquidator may sell the goods, or a sufficient part of
them, for the purpose of satisfying the charge.

(3)   If under an execution in respect of a judgment for a sum
exceeding £500 a company's goods are sold or money is

paid in order to avoid sale, the sheriff shall deduct the costs of the execution from the proceeds of sale or the monies paid and retain the balance for 14 days.

(4)   If within that time notice is served on the sheriff of a petition for the winding-up of the company having been presented or of a meeting having been called at which there is to be proposed a resolution for voluntary winding-up, and an order is made or a resolution passed (as the case may be), the sheriff shall pay the balance to the liquidator, who is entitled to retain it as against the execution creditor.

(5)   The rights conferred by this section on the liquidator may be set aside by the court in favour of the creditor to such extent and subject to such terms as the court thinks fit.

Section 252(2)

An interim order has the effect that, during the period for which it is in force:

(a)   no bankruptcy petition relating to the debtor may be presented or proceeded with, and

(b)   no other proceedings, and no execution or other legal process, may be commenced or continued against the debtor or his property except with the leave of the court.

Section 254

(1)   At any time when an application under s.253 for an interim order is pending, the court may stay any action, execution or other legal process against the property or person of the debtor.

(2)   Any court in which proceedings are pending against an individual may, on proof that an application under that section has been made in respect of that individual, either stay the proceedings or allow them to continue on such terms as it thinks fit.

Section 258 (4)
The meeting shall not approve any proposal or modification which affects the right of a secured creditor of the debtor to enforce his security, except with the concurrence of the creditor concerned.

Section 262

(1)   Subject to this section, an application to the court may be made, by any of the persons specified below, on one or both of the following grounds, namely -

(a)   that a voluntary arrangement approved by a creditors' meeting summoned under s.237 unfairly prejudices the interests of a creditor of the debtor;

(b)   that there has been some material irregularity at or in relation to such a meeting.

(4)   Where on an application under this section the court is satisfied as to either of the grounds mentioned in s.(1), it may do one or both of the following, namely -

(a)   revoke or suspend any approval given by the meeting;

(b)   give a direction to any person for the summoning of a further meeting of the debtor's creditors to consider any revised proposal he may make or, in a case falling within subs.(1)(b), to reconsider his original proposal.

Section 268

(1)   For the purposes of s.267(2)(c), the debtor appears to be unable to pay a debt if, but only if, the debt is payable immediately and either -

(a)   the petitioning creditor to whom the debt is owed has served on the debtor a demand (known as "the statutory demand") in the prescribed form requiring him to pay the debt or to secure or compound for it to the satisfaction of the creditor, at least three weeks have elapsed since the demand was served and the demand has been neither complied with nor set aside in accordance with the rules, or

(b)   execution or other process issued in respect of the debt on a judgment or order of any court in favour of the petitioning creditors to whom the debt is owed, has been returned unsatisfied in whole or in part.

Section 278
The bankruptcy of an individual against whom a bankruptcy order has been made -

(a)   commences with the day on which the order is made, and
(b)   continues until the individual is discharged under the following provisions of this Chapter.

Section 285
(1)   At any time when proceedings on a bankruptcy petition are pending or an individual has been adjudged bankrupt the court may stay any action, execution or other legal process against the property or person of the debtor or, as the case may be, of the bankrupt.
(2)   Any court in which proceedings are pending against any individual may, on proof that a bankruptcy petition has been presented in respect of that individual or that he is an undischarged bankrupt, either stay the proceedings or allow them to continue on such terms as it thinks fit.
(3)   After the making of a bankruptcy order no person who is a creditor of the bankrupt in respect of a debt provable in the bankruptcy shall -

(a)   have any remedy against the property or person of the bankrupt in respect of that debt, or

(b)   before the discharge of the bankrupt, commence
        any action or other legal proceedings against the
        bankrupt except with the leave of the court and on
        such terms as the court may impose.

Section 286
(1)   The court may, if it is shown to be necessary for the
        protection of the debtor's property, at any time after the
        presentation of a bankruptcy petition and before making
        a bankruptcy order, appoint the official receiver to be
        interim receiver of the debtor's property.
(2)   Where the court has, on a debtor's petition, appointed an
        insolvency practitioner under s.273 and it is shown to the
        court as mentioned in subs.(1) of this section, the court
        may, without making a bankruptcy order, appoint that
        practitioner, instead of the official receiver, to be interim
        receiver of the debtor's property.

Section 346
(1)   Subject to s.285 in Chapter II (restrictions on proceedings
        and remedies) and to the following provisions of this
        section, where the creditor of any person who is adjudged
        bankrupt has, before the commencement of the
        bankruptcy -

        (a)   issued execution against the goods or land of that
                person, or
        (b)   attached a debt due to that person from another
                person,

        that creditor is not entitled, as against the official
        receiver or trustee of the bankrupt's estate, to retain the
        benefit of the execution or attachment, or any sums paid
        to avoid it, unless the execution or attachment was
        completed, or the sums paid, before the commencement
        of the bankruptcy.
(2)   Subject as follows, where the goods of a person have been
        taken in execution, then, before the completion of the
        execution notice is given to the sheriff or other officer

charged with the execution that that person has been adjudged bankrupt

(a) the sheriff or other officer shall on request deliver to the official receiver or trustee of the bankrupt's estate the goods and any money seized or recovered in part satisfaction of the execution, but

(b) the costs of the execution are a first charge on the goods or money so delivered and the official receiver or trustee may sell the goods or sufficient part of them for the purpose of satisfying the charge.

(3) Subject to subs.(6) below, where -

(a) under an execution in respect of a judgment exceeding such sum as may be prescribed for the purposes of this subsection, the goods of any person are sold or money paid in order to avoid a sale, and

(b) before the end of the period of 14 days beginning with the day of the sale or payment the sheriff or other officer charged with the execution is given notice that a bankruptcy petition has been presented in relation to that person, and

(c) a bankruptcy order is or has been made on that petition,

the balance of the proceeds of sale or money paid, after deducting the costs of execution, shall (in priority to the claim of the execution creditor) be comprised in the bankrupt's estate.

(4) Accordingly, in the case of an execution in respect of a judgment for the sum exceeding the sum prescribed for the purposes of subs.(3), the sheriff or other officer charged with the execution -

(a) shall not dispose of the balance mentioned in subs.(3) at any time within the 14 days so mentioned or while there is pending a bankruptcy petition of which he has been given notice under that subsection, and

(b)   shall pay that balance, where by virtue of that subsection it is comprised in the bankrupt's estate, to the official receiver or (if there is one) to the trustee of that estate.

(5)   For the purposes of this section -

(a)   an execution against goods is completed by seizure and sale or by the making of a charging order under s.1 of the Charging Orders Act 1979;

(b)   an execution against land is completed by seizure, by the appointment of a receiver or by the making of a charging order under that section;

(c)   an attachment of a debt is completed by the receipt of the debt.

(6)   The rights conferred by subss.(1) to (3) on the official receiver or the trustee may, to such extent and on such terms as it thinks fit, be set aside by the court in favour of the creditor who has issued the execution or attached the debt.

(7)   Nothing in this section entitles the trustee of the bankrupt's estate to claim goods from a person who has acquired them in good faith under a sale by a sheriff or other officer charged with the execution.

(8)   Neither subs.(2) nor subs.(3) applies in relation to any execution against property which has been acquired by or has devolved upon the bankrupt since the commencement of the bankruptcy, unless, at the time the execution is issued or before it has been completed -

(a)   the property has been or is claimed for the bankrupt's estate under s.307 (after-acquired property), and

(b)   a copy of the notice given under that section has been or is served on the sheriff or other officer charged with the execution.

CHAPTER 8

Rent, Rates & Taxes

LANDLORD'S CLAIM FOR RENT

By the Landlord and Tenant Act, 1709, s.1 (Statute 8 Anne ch.14)

"No goods or chattels whatsoever, lying or being in or upon any messuage, land or tenements, which are or shall be leased for life or lives, term of years, at will or otherwise, shall be liable to be taken by virtue of any execution, on any pretence whatever, unless the party at whose suit the execution is sued out, shall, before the removal of such goods from off said premises, by virtue of any execution or extent, pay to the landlord of the said premises or his bailiff, all such sums or sums of money as are or shall be due for rent for the said premises at the time of taking such goods or chattels by virtue of such execution; provided the said arrears of rent do not amount to more than one year's rent; and in case the said arrears shall exceed one year's rent, then the said party, at whose suit the execution is sued out, paying the said landlord or his bailiff one year's rent, may proceed to execute his judgment, as he might have done before the making of this Act, and the Sheriff or other officer is hereby empowered and required to pay to the plaintiff as well the money so paid for rent as the execution money."

The landlord is entitled to claim priority over an execution creditor, other than the Crown, for up to one year's rent which has accrued due (has become payable) prior to the execution being levied on effects within the premises to which the rent relates (the demised premises). Rent payable in advance may be claimed, provided that the date of accrual was prior to that of the seizure by the Sheriff.

The tenancy must exist at the time of the seizure, thus where the tenancy has determined prior to the seizure by the Sheriff, the landlord cannot be entitled to claim arrears from the Sheriff (*Hodgson v. Gascoigne* (1821) 5 B & Ald 88).

If the Sheriff is given notice of up to one year's rent due, he should secure the rent before removing the goods; failure to do so will render him liable to the landlord (*Gawler v. Chaplin* (1848) 18 LT Ex 42). The measure of damages is *prima facie* the amount of the rent due. The Sheriff may reduce them to the real value of the goods but not necessarily to the sum they fetched at forced sale (*Thomas v. Mirehouse* (1887) 36 WR 104).

However, if the rent is paid by the judgment creditor, the warrant may proceed for both rent and judgment.

There is no obligation to enquire if there are arrears of rent (*Re MacKenzie, ex parte Sheriff of Hertfordshire* (1889) 81 LT 214).

The statute does not apply to executions at the suit of the landlord (*Taylor v. Lanyon* (1830) 6 Bing 536).

The statute applies to tenancies for a term of one year or more. Where tenancies are for shorter terms, the rent for which the Sheriff is liable is no more than the rent for four terms. That is, four weeks rent where the tenancy is weekly, four months rent where the tenancy is by the month, (s.67 Execution Act, 1844 and similarly s.102 County Court Act, 1984).

Notice of Rent Due

The duty to deal with rent does not arise until notice of outstanding rent has been served but it should be noted that informal notice has been considered to be sufficient. (*Waring v. Dewberry* (1718) 1 Str 97); Colyer & Speer (1820) 4 Moore 473; *Smith v. Russell* (1811) 3 Taunt 400). However the Court of Appeal in *Thomas v. Mirehouse, (supra)* considered that proper notice was necessary. The Sheriff is entitled to enquire as to the truth of the claim and, if possible, should inspect the lease (*Augustien v. Challis* (1847) 17 LT Ex 73).

If the tenant does not pay the arrears, the Officer must approach the creditor for the rent before removing goods. Should the creditor not pay, the Officer must withdraw. There is a recommended form of notice to the creditor for use by the Officer in such a case, at the end of this section.

Duties of the Sheriff

Lord Esher, MR, considering the duties of the Sheriff, said:

> "Even if there are goods upon the demised premises of the value many times exceeding the amount of the rent due, his duty is the same. He must refuse to sell the smallest part of the goods until the claim of the landlord is satisfied.... He must apply to the execution creditor for the sum which is necessary." (*Thomas v. Mirehouse,* (1887) (*supra*).

Identity of the Tenant

It is essential that the tenant and the judgment debtor be one and the same. If they differ, the Sheriff is not liable to the landlord. It was established that where a landlord claimed rent from the Sheriff under s.1 Landlord & Tenant Act 1709, there must exist an immediate relationship of landlord and tenant between the landlord and the execution debtor. Where the tenants are the directors of a debtor company there is no such relationship and the Sheriff is not liable for the rent in an execution against the debtor company (*Eastcheap Alimentary Products Ltd* (1936) LT 155, 521).

By analogy, where an execution is against S.... and J.... Limited and the landlord claims rent due from S.... and J.... (a firm), the Sheriff is not liable for the rent.

Distress by Landlord

The priority of the landlord is to give him protection when he loses his right of distress. Distraint for rent may not be made on goods already in the custody of the law, thus once possession has been taken under a *fi:fa* the landlord has only the remedy given him by the act (*Peacock v. Purvis* (1820) 5 Moore CP 79; *Wright v. Dewes* (1834) 3 LJ KB 181, etc).

One aspect which may affect execution is the description of assets available for seizure under either a levy or a distress. Whilst the Sheriff may only proceed against goods and chattels of the debtor and must acknowledge third party claims, the landlord is permitted, with certain exceptions, to proceed against all goods on the demised premises. If the Officer receives claims which are admitted by the judgment creditor he must withdraw from possession of those items; they may then become available for distress by the landlord (*Cropper v. Warner* (1883) CAB EL 152; *Cooper v. Asprey* (1863) 11 WR 641).

Dispute as to Rent Due

The Sheriff may not interplead on a landlord's claim for rent (*Bateman v. Farnsworth* (1860) 2 LT 390; *Clark v. Lord* (1833) 2 Dowl PC 55,227).

A claim for rent is the one claim the merits of which must be decided by the Sheriff and not by the creditor. If the Officer proceeds in the face of a claim for rent he is liable in an action for damages by the landlord.

Poundage on Sale

Should a sale proceed for both the rent and the judgment, the Sheriff cannot deduct poundage from the rent recovered, the landlord is entitled to the full amount of the rent without abatement. Nevertheless poundage is chargeable, and it can be retained from the realization if more than sufficient is sold to satisfy the rent due (*Davies v. Edmunds* (1843) 13 LJ Ex 1; *Gore v. Grafton* (1725) 1 Stra 643; *Williams v. Lewsey* (1831) 8 Bing 28).

General

The Officer's obligation to deal with the landlord arises only when the goods are to be removed from the demised premises. It does not prevent the Officer from levying and receiving monies under the warrant provided that he does not remove the goods for a projected sale. Nor does it apply to a sale of effects remaining on the premises as the landlord would still have his right of distress after the sale, but this procedure may be impractical unless the sale is to a party who does not propose to remove the goods from the premises and is prepared to deal with the outstanding rent (*White v. Binstead* (1853) 22 LJCP 115; *Smallman v. Pollard* (1844) 6 M & G 1001).

County Court Execution

Section 102, County Court Act, 1984 makes the Bailiff liable to the landlord for up to four weeks rent where the tenancy is weekly, up to two terms where the tenancy is for any other term less than a year, and in any other case, up to a year's rent. The same act permits the recovery of additional fees where the effects are sold to recover rent due, the distress to be regarded as though it were an execution of the court.

Insolvency

The extent of the landlord's claim for rent due may be reduced to six months should bankruptcy intervene. The dates are relevant and reference should be made to the Insolvency Act, 1986, s.347. But the making of an Interim Order under the act against a debtor does not debar a landlord from distraining for his rent because a distress for rent is not a legal process of a judicial or adjudicative nature (*McMullen & Sons Ltd v. Cerrone* (1993) *The Times*, June 10).

Procedure

After levy, proceed unless notice is given of rent due. If there is notice, contact the landlord or his agent to ascertain:

1.   Is the tenancy still in existence.
2.   Who is the tenant?
3.   What is the amount of rent due?
4.   To what period does it relate?
5.   When did it fall due?

If the Officer is satisfied that rent is indeed due from the debtor to his landlord, and that it accrued due before the date of the seizure, then:

6.   Seek payment of the rent from the creditor.
7.   If no monies are paid specifically in respect of the rent, withdraw from possession.
8.   If the creditor deposits the rent with the Officer, proceed to sell for both rent and the execution.

Form of Notice by the Sheriff to the Execution Creditor that rent is owing and requiring that payment be made by such creditor

In the High Court of Justice
...................................Division

Between   ....Plaintiff

and

....Defendant

Take notice that the sum of £............ is due and owing from the above named defendant to his landlord .... of .... for (one year's, or half year's, or quarter's) rent due on .... and in respect of the premises situate at .... in the county of... now in the occupation of the said defendant, and upon which certain of the goods and chattels have been seized by the Sheriff of .... under the writ of fieri facias issued in this action. Now I do hereby, as the agent of the said Sheriff and on his behalf give you notice that unless the above named plaintiff do forthwith pay the arrears of rent due to the said landlord, either to him or to his bailiff, pursuant to statute in such case made and provided, the said Sheriff will withdraw from possession of the said goods and chattels under the said writ.

Dated this

signed..............................(agent to the Sheriff)

To the above named plaintiff and to
.... his solicitor or agent.

RATES

The metamorphosis from Rates to Council Tax via Community Charge has not, so far as the Sheriff is concerned, altered the position vis-a-vis himself and a person distraining for any outstanding tax.

Unlike unpaid rent, outstanding rates do not take precedence over an execution.

The Local Authority may authorize distraint for unpaid rates, distraining on the goods of the rate-payer wherever those goods may be found. Distress is not restricted to the address applicable to the rate charge.

If a Bailiff has distrained under a Rates Distress warrant (which is issued following the making of a Liability Order by the Magistrates Court), the goods are not available for seizure under an execution until the distress is completed or abandoned. The Officer cannot levy on goods already seized under another process and, by analogy, no more can the Rates Bailiff distrain after seizure by the Sheriff because the goods are in the custody of the law.

Goods which are exempt from distress for rates include those already in the custody of the landlord for rent and those taken into possession by the Inland Revenue for taxes. It has been suggested that the position as to goods taken in execution is uncertain but that would appear to contradict the foregoing.

Priority

Priority is established by virtue of the respective dates and times of levy or distraint.

A person distraining for rates is obliged to leave on the premises a copy of the Notice of Seizure (as in a rent distress).

A judgment debtor should be able to advise the Officer if there is a prior distress for rates. A rates distress can only be executed on the same assets, goods and chattels, available for seizure under a *fi:fa*, being assets of the debtor and not including those of third parties, nor those of the ratepayer's family, nor those supplied under retention of title or hire purchase agreements.

For further information as to Rates Distress, see "Distress for Rent & Rates & Community Charge" and "Ryde on Rating".

TAXES

By the Taxes Management Act, 1970, s.62 as amended by s.153, Finance Act 1989:

"1.   If at any time at which any goods or chattels belonging to any person (in this section referred to as 'the person in default') are liable to be taken by virtue of any execution or other process, warrant or authority whatever, or by virtue of any assignment, on any account or pretence whatever, except at the suit of the landlord for rent, the person in default is in arrears in respect of any such sums as are referred to in subs.(1A) below, the goods and chattels may not be so taken unless on demand made by the collector the persons at whose suit the execution or seizure is made, or to whom the assignment was made, pays or causes to be paid to the collector, before sale or removal of the goods or chattels, all such sums as have fallen due at or before the date of seizure."

(A)   The sums referred to in subs.(1) above are -

(a)   "sums due from the person in default on account of deductions of income tax from emoluments paid during the period of 12 months next before the date of seizure, being deductions which the person in default was liable to make under s.203 of the principal Act (pay as you earn) less the amount of the repayments of income tax which he was liable to make during that period; and

(b)   sums due from the person in default in respect of deductions required to be made by him for that period under s.559 of the principal Act (sub-contractors in the construction industry)."

The Inland Revenue, before the 1989 amendment to the Act, had the right to a prior claim for up to one year's tax except under distress for rent. The Collector of Taxes may now only call upon the Sheriff to pay taxes due for deductions of PAYE and under the "lump" before any removal of effects may take place. This right is similar to that granted to the landlord in respect of unpaid rent. The Act does not prevent the Officer from entering into possession, nor does it prevent the debtor satisfying the warrant by payment. The priority of the collector does not extend to monies in the hands of the Sheriff or his Officer.

Duties of the Sheriff

If the Officer is advised that there are taxes due, even though there has been no distress, he must contact the appropriate tax office and seek a formal claim for the tax.

If a claim is made, the Officer must seek payment from the creditor before proceeding to a removal. If the creditor is not prepared to satisfy the tax demand, the Officer must withdraw immediately.

Unfortunately, the willingness to provide information varies from office to office of the Inland Revenue. One can only assume that if a request for details of taxes due is made to the correct office and none are forthcoming, the Officer may proceed with the warrant. However, it is prudent to record the request and refusal in writing.

Distress by Collector

More commonly, the Officer will find that the Collector has distrained on the effects. The Officer cannot proceed under his warrant as the effects are not available for seizure. In such cases, the Officer should obtain full details of the distress, a copy of the schedule of goods distrained and confirmation that the distress remains in force. A report to this effect is then made to the creditor's solicitor.

Monies Paid by Debtor

The debtor may still satisfy the warrant. There is no obligation for monies to be applied to the distress and the warrant in date order of issue. That priority applies only to judgments and orders, not to administrative procedures.

VALUE ADDED TAX

The authority of HM Customs & Excise to claim VAT was contained in the Finance Act, 1972 where it was stated in s.33 and subsequently re-enacted in VAT Act 1994:

"Tax due from any persons shall be recoverable as a debt due to the Crown".

It is the usual practice of Customs & Excise to recover arrears of VAT by means of distress.

The right of distress was conferred on the Commissioners by s.33, Finance Act, 1972 as amplified in VAT General Regulations 1974, (SI 1974 No.1379) and Regulation 65, Value Added Tax (General) Regulations 1985 (SI 1985 No.886) as amended 1993. The distress is restricted to goods and chattels of the taxpayer and the usual rules applicable to distress apply.

A distress is not a "legal process of a judicial or adjudicative nature" (see *McMullen & Sons Ltd v. Cerrone* (1993) *The Times*, June 10). It appears therefore that unless the amount of VAT due has become a debt of record, that is, the debt has become a judgment debt, the Customs & Excise cannot claim Crown preference for a projected distress over a subject's execution. (See ch.2, Crown Priority for a discussion of this subject.)

In practice, if the Officer is advised that there is VAT owing, he should first ascertain if the Customs & Excise have distrained. If there is a distress, contact should be made with the local Collector to confirm priority of seizure dates, that the distress remains in force and to ascertain the items distrained. If the response is that the seizure date is prior to that of the Sheriff's and covers all effects of value, the Officer may not proceed until the distress is removed and should report to the creditor accordingly.

If Customs & Excise have issued a writ of *fi:fa* for their debt, that writ will take priority over any other not at the suit of the Crown in the Sheriff's hands.

CHAPTER 9

Sale of Goods

Where an execution remains unsatisfied, it is the duty of the Officer to proceed to sale without delay. There is no requirement to delay sale for a period of five days as is mandatory under distress or County Court warrant.

The sale must be by public auction unless the items offered are being sold under an execution for less than £20. The sale must be publicly advertised "on, and during three days, preceding the day of sale", (s.138A(1) Supreme Court Act, 1981 following s.145, Bankruptcy Act, 1883).

Although there is no requirement to do so, the Officer should ensure that catalogues of the sale are sent to the debtor and to the solicitor for the creditor in sufficient time to allow either to attend the sale.

However, the Sheriff may apply to the Court for permission to sell by private treaty if he is of the opinion a better price may be obtained thereby, (s.138A(2), *ibid.*, and RSC, O.47, r.6).

Private Sales

Where the goods taken are of a specialized nature or where they may have a value to the debtor's colleagues or family, it may be in the best interests of all parties for the auction process to be bypassed and the consent of the Court sought to sell privately and, on occasion, without advertisement.

When reaching a decision as to whether a better price may be obtained by private sale rather than by auction, the costs of the removal and storage as well as the probable costs of the application should be borne in mind. It is the nett result which is relevant.

Application for leave is made by summons together with a short affidavit of the circumstances and may be made by the Sheriff, the execution creditor or by the execution debtor. If the Sheriff is not the applicant, the applicant is entitled to obtain from the Sheriff a list, known as the Sheriff's list, of all other execution creditors of the debtor who must also be served with the summons. The Sheriff's List must also be produced to the Court on the hearing. The debtor or any judgment creditor may object on the application. For detailed practice see *Supreme Court Practice*, O.46, r.6.

The normal order made is permissive and not mandatory, so the Sheriff "may" sell privately, he "need" not do so. The Court may ask for details of any offers which have been received. Where it is considered advisable for advertisements to be placed in newspapers seeking offers, a provisional order may be granted subject to the Sheriff's solicitors returning to the Court when firm offers are received. This practice is of use when dealing with quality cars, a market in which buyers expect to take delivery without delay.

The costs of the application may be added to the judgment and so are recoverable under the *fi:fa*. The commission allowed on a private sale is not the same as that allowed on auction. (See ch.16, SHERIFF'S FEES).

The Sheriff cannot make a valid contract for sale of goods of a debtor against whom he holds a *fi:fa* until he has actually seized the goods, (*ex parte Hall, in re Townsend* (1880) 28 WR 556) but the goods may be sold to the execution creditor, (*ex parte Villars* (1874) LR 9 Ch 432).

Private Sales - Rent or Taxes Due

If a sale by private treaty takes place, it may be that effects are not removed from the premises. The position of the Sheriff may then become confused if there are outstanding taxes or rent. In order to protect the Officer, the Court may incorporate in the Order the following: "and that the Sheriff do pay out of the proceeds of such sale the rent due and the Queen's Taxes if any."

Selling for Value

The Sheriff is obliged to ensure that a realistic price is received for the goods offered. The Court may set aside a sale it considers to have been badly advertised and where the sale was at undervalue (*Edge v. Kavanagh* (1884) 24 LR Ir 1; *Barnard v. Leigh* (1815) 1 Stark 43).

However, if the sale fails through lack of reasonable bids and the Sheriff re-offers the goods more than once, subsequently accepting the best bid made, the Court may accept the result (*Cramer v. Murphy* (1887) 20 LR Ir 572 and see also ch.13 under *Venditioni Exponas*).

In *The Observer v. Gordon* (1983) 1 WLR 1008, Glidewell, J drew attention to the need for the Sheriff to ensure that the auctioneers chosen to conduct the sale were competent in that field. It was argued that specialized items, in that instance grand pianos, may not achieve the best price possible when sold by an auctioneer whose main market was antiques or furniture. Applying this dictum, Officers should enquire as to the normal market of the auctioneers and should be prepared to use the services of several auctioneers if necessary, particularly those who tend to specialize.

Sale on Debtor's premises

The Sheriff has no authority to hold an auction sale on the debtor's premises without the debtor's consent (*Watson v. Murray & Co.* (1955) 1 All ER 350).

Sale of Farming Stock

The Sale of Farming Stock Act, 1816, restricted the ability to sell certain stock and crops where the debtor is a tenant of a farm property. The Sheriff is bound by covenants made in the lease between the tenant and his landlord. Reference should be made to pp.318 to 323 of *Mather* 3rd edn.

Several Sales

Sales conducted over several days are deemed to be one transaction (*re Villars, ex parte Rogers* (1874) 22 WR 397, 603). The commission allowed to the auctioneer relates to the entire sale, the varying scale does not apply to each and every sale.

Title in Goods

The property in the goods seized remains with the debtor

until sale but subject to the security of the judgment creditor (*in re Clarke, ex parte Williams* (1898) 78 LT 275; *Slater v. Pinder* (1872) 20 WR 441).

As to warranty of title,

> "the Sheriff does not impliedly warrant his title, or warrant the purchaser against eviction, he merely promises that he does not, at the time he sells, know of any defect in his authority, or that he has not the right to sell." (*Addison on Contracts*, 11th edn, p.560).

The purchaser of goods from the Sheriff, following a sale under a writ of *fi:fa*, acquires a title which is good against a trustee in bankruptcy. The advent of the Insolvency Act 1986 removed the sale of goods as an available act of bankruptcy. Bankruptcy now commences with the making of the Order (s.278), thus the trustee may not attempt to set aside prior transactions of this nature, (Insolvency Act, 1986, ss.183, 346).

Where goods are in the possession of the debtor at the time of seizure and where no third party claim to ownership is made, the purchaser from the Sheriff acquires a good title. The Sheriff is protected from an action for selling such goods unless it is proved that the Sheriff had notice or might by making reasonable enquiries have ascertained that the goods were those of a third party, (s.138B, Supreme Court Act, 1981 re-enacting s.15, Bankruptcy & Deeds of Arrangement Act, 1913 and see also *Dyal Singh v. Kenyan Insurance Ltd* (1954) 1 All ER 847; *Curtis v. Mahoney* (1951) 1 KB 736).

Sale after Bankruptcy Order

If the Official Receiver or Trustee fails to give a request

to deliver to the Sheriff under s.346, Insolvency Act 1986, the Sheriff is still bound to sell the goods in his hands but the execution creditor may not derive any benefit from the sale, the proceeds of which must be paid to the Official Receiver or Trustee (*Woolford's Trustee v. Levy* (1892) 1 QB 772).

Stopping the Sale

The sale must be stopped by the Officer whenever sufficient monies are realized. Should the sale continue, the debtor would be entitled to sue for wrongful disposal of his effects (*Batchelor v. Vyse* (1834) 4 M & Scott 552).

VAT on Sale Proceeds

The Finance Act, 1972, sch.2, para.2 states:

"Where the goods acquired or produced by a taxable person in the course of a business carried on by him are, under any power exercisable by another person, sold by the other person in or towards satisfaction of a debt owed by the taxable person they shall be deemed to be supplied by the taxable person in the course of that business."

The Value Added Tax General Regulations, 1974, para.52 state:

"Where goods are deemed to be supplied by a taxable person by virtue of para.2 of sch.2 to the Act, the person selling the goods, whether or not he is registered under the Act, shall within 21 days of the sale -

(a)   furnish to the Controller a statement showing -
   (i)   his name and address and, if registered, his registration number,
   (ii)   the name and address and registration number of the person whose goods were sold,
   (iii) the date of the sale,
   (iv)   the description and quantity of the goods sold, and
   (v)   the amount for which they were sold and the amount of the tax chargeable.

(b)   pay the amount of the tax due and
(c)   send to the person whose goods were sold a copy of the statement referred to in a) above,

and the person selling the goods and the person whose goods were sold shall exclude from any return which either or both may be required to furnish under these regulations the tax chargeable on that supply of goods."

Accounting for the Proceeds and the VAT

The date of the receipt of the monies is taken as being the date of the sale and the auctioneer is acting for the Sheriff, thus a sale by the auctioneer is a sale by the Sheriff.

The VAT arising on the sale should be paid to the VAT authorities in Southend on Sea, Essex, using their form 833. Payment of this tax is to be made within 21 days of the sale. It is normal for the auctioneers to forward these monies direct, rather than accounting to the Officer for the gross proceeds.

Surplus Sale Proceeds

As seizure and sale by the Sheriff is no longer an act of bankruptcy, there would appear to be no obligation to hold any surplus proceeds for a period of three months. If the sale is sufficient to satisfy the execution and the allowable costs, any surplus should be refunded to the debtor after being held for the 14 days required by the provisions of the Insolvency Act, 1986.

The Auctioneer, the Sheriff and Consumer Protection

The Consumer Protection Act 1987 introduced a general safety requirement concerning the sale of goods and by that Act made it a criminal offence to supply goods which are unsafe. The Act divided goods into two categories, regulated and unregulated. In the case of the first it is an absolute offence to sell goods that are unsafe, in the second it is possible to exclude liability provided that sufficient notice is given to the buyer.

An auctioneer is considered by recent statute to be a supplier of secondhand goods. The term "supplier" can include both principal and agent. The auctioneer is therefore governed by the provisions of the Trades Descriptions Acts, Consumer Protection Act and the multitude of regulations and orders made over the past few years concerning consumer safety. The auctioneer can no longer expect to rely on the maxim "let the buyer beware", or on any conditions he may specify himself in his conditions of sale, to avoid liability under these regulations and statutory requirements. The Sheriff is often in the position of a principal in these transactions and can become equally liable in cases where Trading

Standards Departments enforce regulations in respect of supply of goods, possessing or exposing goods for sale.

Most matters enforced by Trading Standards Officers entail penalties enforced by prosecution of the offenders and it is easy for the Sheriff, Under Sheriff or the Officer to become embroiled in a criminal prosecution by accident, so to speak. It has been found in practice that Trading Standards Officers, who are organised on a county basis, have widely differing views as to their enforcement procedures, and widely differing interpretations of the standards and indeed categories of the goods with which they deal, although they endeavour to reach a broadly similar approach throughout the country.

To mention just a part of the list of goods covered by regulations, there are requirements laid down for the safety of the following categories of goods which must not be sold, exposed for sale and, in some cases, even possessed, if found to be unsafe or in an unsatisfactory condition:

Furniture - particularly upholstered furniture manufactured between the years 1950 and 1988, which must have coverings which satisfy fire resistance requirements. Such furniture must have in place a permanent label stating that the item complies with the regulations. Furniture manufactured before 1950 is exempt from these requirements, although upholstered antique furniture that has been recovered or re-upholstered more recently may be required to comply so far as the new work is concerned. These rules in effect made secondhand upholstered furniture manufactured after 1950 virtually unsaleable at auction.

Fireguards. Regulations exist covering sizes of apertures.

Gas appliances must comply with various regulations and standards, EN 30, BS 5386 etc.

Electrical appliances. All standards must be complied with. Plugs, if fitted, must comply with wiring standards and labelling with Kite marks. Auctioneers, in consequence, normally remove all plugs from electrical goods before sale. Cables must conform to the Electrical Appliances (Colour Code) Regulations 1969. Red, green and black wires are NOT allowed. All appliances should be inspected for safety before sale.

Oil heaters are subject to much regulation and must bear statutory warnings concerning their operation.

Toys, where secondhand, must be safe. New toys should bear the CE mark and name and address of the first supplier. The definition of toy includes any product or material designed or intended for use in play by children under the age of 14 years. The following however are not toys: Christmas decorations, detailed scale models for adult collectors, sports equipment, folk dolls for collectors, puzzles with over 500 pieces, air guns, air pistols, slings and catapults, darts with metallic points, electrical equipment operating at over 24 volts, fashion jewellery and reproductions of real fire arms.

Prams, pushchairs and carry-cots must comply with BS 4139, 4792 or 3381 respectively, and must be safe at the time of supply. They must bear warnings regarding their proper use.

Carry-cot stands must have a permanently fixed label stating the maximum size of carry-cot it is designed to bear, and be within laid down dimensions.

Crash helmets and visors. Helmets must comply with BS 6658. Visors must carry the kitemark and be manufactured to BS 4110.

Bunk beds must comply with requirements concerning dimensions of safety rails, gap sizes, etc.

Asbestos or products containing asbestos must carry a specific warning label.

Childrens' Clothing is subject to some regulation, for example: Childrens' Clothing (Hood Cords) Regulations, 1976, make it an offence to supply or possess for supply outer garments for children that have a hood with a pull cord fastening.

Cooking Utensils must comply with 1972 regulations on safety of metal coatings containing lead.

Ceramic wares such as plates must comply with BS 6748 limits on metal release.

Videos are subject to labelling requirements following the Video Recordings Act 1984. The legislation provides for a film classification system to outlaw or restrict the sale or hire of the most violent and sexually explicit films and to classify all other material as to its suitability for viewing in the home by persons of various ages. The act applies to any person who supplies or offers to supply video works. The seller or supplier is expected to make a detailed cross-check of the containers and cassettes in every case. To avoid difficulty, Officers removing such items for sale and auctioneers selling such items should ensure that they have a good knowledge of the classification categories and requirements as to labelling and packaging.

It is an offence amongst others, to supply, offer to supply or have in possession for supply an uncertified video recording. Any video having a "Restricted 18" classification is only allowed to be supplied in a licensed sex shop. It is therefore unlikely that the Sheriff will be able to deal with such items.

Prosecutions have also been instituted against auctioneers (and the Sheriff) concerning alleged misdescription of goods in auction catalogues contrary to the Trades Description Acts. In producing catalogues for sales, the utmost care must be taken to avoid such unpleasantness particularly where auctioneers compile catalogues directly from removal lists or Officers' inventories.

CHAPTER 10

Abortive Executions

A proportion of the writs issued to the Sheriff will prove unsuccessful as a result of directions to old, vacant or incorrect addresses, incorrect description of debtors, directions to premises where there are no effects available for seizure despite a connexion with the debtor and so on. The Officer is bound by the command contained in the warrant and should not proceed to alternative addresses unless instructed to do so by the judgment creditor. Should he do so without specific instructions he is at risk.

Nevertheless, the creditor is entitled to expect that proper inquiries be made at the given address and that the Officer reports promptly. It may be that those inquiries reveal alternative premises at which effects may be found. The creditor may then re-direct the Officer or issue a concurrent writ if appropriate.

Reporting

It is customary for the creditor to receive a full report of the Officer's attendance especially when the Officer has obtained information which might assist in the recovery of the judgment debt at alternative addresses or by alternative means. However, the Officer is not an inquiry agent, his report should be confined to what actually took place when he attended and the steps he took to confirm the information obtained.

Apart from the actual attendance, the Officer should consider the local directories which are available and which may allow him to confirm information he has been given. The telephone directory and the Electoral Roll are obvious sources of information. The latter may be consulted in libraries, post offices and certain police stations.

Where the Officer has met with the debtor under previous executions, he should not rely on his experience in those matters, especially in cases where that experience relates to a matter which proved abortive at some time in the past. A new writ must always be attended upon to confirm that the situation has not altered.

Sheriff's Returns in Abortive Cases

In order to pursue other methods of execution, creditors frequently require the Sheriff to make his return in the case of an abortive execution. The usual return made will be, "No goods, execution unsatisfied in whole or in part", but the Sheriff must be careful in matters where he has been unable to make any contact with the debtor. In *re A Debtor* (No.340 of 1992), *The Debtor v. First National Commercial Bank Plc & anor* (1994) 3 All ER 269 the court made a clear distinction between a writ that was returned "unsatisfied" and a writ that was returned "unexecuted" with adverse results in that case for the creditor who had sought to found a bankruptcy petition on the return. It seems reasonable to us to suggest therefore, that the Sheriff should recite a full statement of the attendances made in cases where no contact has been made with the debtor and the writ has been countermanded by the execution creditor.

In extension of the principle decided in that case, it is conceivable that a return of "No goods" where the Sheriff is directed to premises which have no material connexion with the debtor, for example, the house of his parents, or an office occupied by his solicitor or accountant, may not be sufficient to found a petition in bankruptcy because the Sheriff is unable to state with certainty that the debtor has been given notice of the execution and has demonstrated the inability or unwillingness to pay required by s.268(1)(b) Insolvency Act 1986.

Charges

Whilst the Sheriff's Scale of Fees is primarily concerned with executions where goods or cash have been taken, there have been successful taxations of accounts rendered following abortive attendances.

These accounts should reflect the reasonable costs of the Officer attending and reporting. The Fee Scale includes under the heading, "Generally":

"... For any duty not otherwise provided for, such sums as one of the Masters of the Supreme Court, or District Registrars of the High Court may upon special application allow."

CHAPTER 11

Accounting

Monies received from the debtor are due to be paid over to the judgment creditor without delay. However, monies received under executions in excess of £500 (Insolvency Proceedings (Monetary Limits) Order 1986 (SI 1986, No.1996)) are to be retained by the Sheriff for a period of 14 days before payment may be made to the creditor, (s.184 and s.346 Insolvency Act, 1986). In deciding whether or not an execution is above this limit, account must also be taken of the Sheriff's charges leviable, (*ex parte Liverpool Loan Co., in re Bullen* (1872) LR Ch 732; *Howes v. Young, Howes v. Stone,* (1876) 1 Ex D 146; *Willey v. Hucks* (1909) 1 KB 760). The cases cited all concerned the operation of s.87, Bankruptcy Act, 1869, which legislation has been carried forward through successive Bankruptcy Acts to the present. See also *Mather* at p.440.

Whilst in the hands of the Sheriff or Officer, the monies are as it were "in suspense". They are not funds of the creditor nor those of the debtor. *Per* Chitty, LJ,

"The result of the authorities apart from the enactment is that the Sheriff holds the money to the use of the judgment creditor and is liable to be sued in an action for the money had and received ... By the enactment referred to the Sheriff is directed to retain the money for 14 days and in the event of bankruptcy supervening the execution creditor loses his right to the money. The effect is to place a temporary embargo or stop on the money. If more technical language is requisite, I say the execution creditor's right to the money is vested, but is liable to be divested. His right to the money is not a contingent right". (*In re Greer, Napper v. Fanshawe* (1895) 2 CH 217).

The effect of insolvency and liquidation is dealt with in Chapter seven but it should be mentioned here that s.184 and s.346 of the Insolvency Act 1986 require the Sheriff to retain the monies for 14 days in case a bankruptcy petition is presented or liquidation commenced. Should either occur, the monies are trapped and will eventually be taken for the benefit of the creditors in general and not particularly for the benefit of the judgment creditor. This divestment does not apply where an Interim Administration Order is applied for, nor when made, (*re Ian Doney*, (1988) Burnley County Court unreported).

The problems arising from the 14 day period have been the subject of several cases, the most notable being *In re Walkden Sheet Metal Co. Ltd* (1959) 3 All ER 333; *Hellyer v. Sheriff of Yorkshire* (1974) 2 All ER 712 and *Marley Tile Co. Ltd v. Burrows* (1978) 3 WLR 641 CA.

These cases established that each payment made to the Sheriff was to be considered separately; each having its own 14 day period. The last mentioned case went further and defined the difference between monies paid under an execution, monies paid to avoid a sale and monies seized. It was decided that monies seized and monies paid under an execution must be held until the whole judgment was completed but monies paid to avoid a sale could be paid to the creditor after 14 days had elapsed.

As the Officer is obliged to proceed to sale if he is not paid, it is reasonable to assume that all payments are made to avoid a sale. Monies recovered from a shop till however, may be considered as being "monies seized".

Statutory Corporations

A corporation or commission established by statute cannot be wound up by a creditor in the Companies Court, (s.718(2) Companies Act 1985). Examples of such bodies include a London Borough and the British Transport Commission, (see the judgment of Lord Denning in *Tamlin v. Hannaford* (1949) 2 All ER 327 CA for a detailed description of the British Transport Commission's legal status). It can only be abolished by statute and, as it is not amenable to the provisions of the Insolvency Acts in that respect, neither is there any need for the provision of the fourteen day embargo. Section 184, Insolvency Act 1986 does not apply to such a body and the Sheriff should pay over any monies received under an execution against such corporation or commission as soon as is reasonably practical.

Payments Received on Account

The date on which monies are received is relevant when calculating the 14 day period. In *Marley Tile Co. Ltd v. Burrows (supra)*, Lord Denning stated that receipt by the Officer was effectively receipt by the Sheriff. He referred to s.167 of the Bankruptcy Act, 1914 (see also s.184 and s.346 Insolvency Act, 1986) which stated, "Sheriff includes any officer charged with the execution of a writ or any other process". By analogy this extends to sale proceeds received by an auctioneer or other appointed agent.

Date of Receipt

Traditionally, it has been the practice to assume the date of payment by the debtor was the date of receipt by the Officer, whether by cash, draft or cheque. However payment by cheque was the subject of an action involving the Inland Revenue in which it was decided the date of receipt was the date the account was actually credited with funds the recipient could use, not the date the cheque was received (*Parkside Leasing v. Smith (Inspector of Taxes)* (1984) *The Times*, November 19).

Payments made by Third Parties

Whilst all monies received from the debtor must be applied to writs in order of priority, payments made by third parties may be allocated to specific executions (*Bower v. Hett* (1895) 73 LT 176). Similarly, as such payments do not deplete the assets of the debtor they are not subject to the provisions of the Insolvency Act, 1986.

"Clients" Account

There is no obligation for the Sheriff to operate a clients' account as such, nor is there any obligation to place monies held on an interest bearing account. The execution creditor has no right to the money until the 14 days have expired. The Sheriff may be required to pay away before the time has expired and the monies must be kept freely available for the purpose. Nevertheless if the monies are retained pending a further Order of the Court, for example an interpleader or an application to have judgment set aside, the funds may be placed on deposit with interest accruing to whoever derives the final benefit.

Notwithstanding the lack of statutory obligation to operate a clients' account, the Officer must ensure that all monies held are capable of identification and capable of separation from the Officer's general account.

Accounting to Creditors

The practice of accounting varies from county to county. In some the Officers account directly. In others the monies are forwarded to the Under Sheriff for onward transmission. It does not matter which system is used provided the creditor receives the monies on the due date. The Officer should not account to the Under Sheriff on the 15th day and the Under Sheriff then account to the creditor on a later day; the transfer of funds between Officer and Under Sheriff should take place earlier if necessary.

Payments may be made "generally on account" of the execution, provided the funds have been held for the required 14 day period and that they fall within the definition of "monies paid to avoid sale". The creditor should apply to the Officer or Under Sheriff for such payments.

CHAPTER 12

Writs of Possession, Delivery, etc

WRIT OF POSSESSION

The writ directs the Sheriff to put the plaintiff into possession of the buildings or land described in the judgment. The warrant directed to the Officer may be in one of two forms, the first where the occupants are identified following a judgment under RSC, O.45, "The defendant do give the plaintiff possession of the land", and the second, where there are "persons unknown" following a judgment under RSC, O.113, "The plaintiff do recover possession of the land".

The writ must contain a specific description of the land of which it is desired to obtain possession (*Thynne v. Sarl* (1891) 64 LT 781). A second writ of possession for the same property may not be issued until the first has been endorsed by the Sheriff to the effect that possession of the whole of the property has not been given to the landlord.

A writ of possession under RSC, O.45 may be combined with a writ of *fi:fa*. A writ of *fi:fa*, in the case of a judgment given against persons unknown, cannot be executed, the party against whom it is sought to levy must be identified with certainty.

Time of Execution

As with a writ of *fi:fa*, there is no period of grace allowed to the defendant or occupant, the writ is one of immediate execution. However, it has been held that the expressions "immediate" or "at once" are to be interpreted as meaning "as soon as is practicable". An application for a mandatory injunction against the Sheriff of Greater London was refused by Knox, J who said "... the expression 'at once' is unfortunate and misleading ... the test is what is reasonably practicable ..." (*Six Arlington Street Investments Ltd v. Persons Unknown* (1986) *The Times*, March 31).

The Sheriff is not entitled to delay the execution because he believes the judgment is bad or that it will be the subject of a stay of execution (*Mason v. Paynter* (1841) 1 QB 974,981).

A return of "Inability to execute" to the writ will always be bad regardless of the practical difficulty of the matter. The Sheriff is entitled to call the *posse comitatus* or power of the county to support him in the execution; no possession warrant is incapable of enforcement.

Warning Occupants

There is no obligation for the Officer to attend to warn the occupants of impending eviction, but it would be most unwise not to do so. The Officer should be aware of the reception he may expect or problems which may arise, and whether special equipment or support is required. Health and Safety at Work requirements appear to demand that the Sheriff takes steps to ensure that his Officers enjoy a safe working environment as far as possible and a preliminary visit to the premises appears to be a necessary precaution in this respect.

Forcing Entry

For the purposes of the execution, entry may be gained by force, as after the judgment it is not the house of the tenant or defendant (*Semaynes Case*, (1604) 77 ER 194).

Use of Force

The Officer is entitled to use reasonable force to eject the occupants. This term is not defined and what is reasonable in ejecting a heavyweight boxer may not be the same as is needed to eject an elderly female.

Occupant's Ill-health

Donaldson, J (as he then was) said that if an Officer declines to execute the writ on the grounds that the occupant is ill he may be held liable as it is not open to him (the Officer) to alter or vary the ruling of the Court (*H.L. Denton and Ors v. Alachouzou* (1978) unreported).

Extent of Writ

The writ extends to the eviction of all persons found upon the premises (*Upton v. Wells* (1589) 1 Leon 145), but not necessarily to the removal of goods and chattels. Whilst this is stated categorically in s.111 of the County Court Act 1984, there is no specific authority in the High Court. However, in *Norwich Union Life Insurance Society v. Preston* (1957) 1 WLR 813, the defendant rather than the Sheriff was ordered to remove the furniture. Also, there appears to be no requirement for the Sheriff to remove animals from the premises, they fall into the same category as the defendant's goods and chattels. The test is not the same as would be applied to a vendor giving "vacant possession" to a purchaser.

Identification of Premises

It is the responsibility of the plaintiff to identify the premises to which the writ relates, and the landlord or his agent must attend to show the actual premises or land and to receive possession. It is a good return to the writ that no one came to point out the premises (see *Mather*, 3rd edn, at p.187; *Connor v. West* (1770) 5 Burr 2673; *Thynne v. Sarl* (1891), *supra*).

The plaintiff may seek an order for possession of the whole area of an estate although only part may be illegally occupied. This is to permit the ejection of the occupants wherever they be within the area at the time of the eviction (*University of Essex v. Djemal and Others* (1980) 2 All ER 742).

Irregular or Wrongful Eviction

Neither the Sheriff nor his Officer is liable in an action for damages for executing a writ of possession according to its tenor or according to either's mistaken view of its effect, nor are they liable if they follow the advice of the landlord's solicitor unless they take an indemnity from the landlord as to that advice (*Williams v. Williams & Nathan* (1937) 2 All ER 559 CA; *Barclays Bank v. Roberts* (1954) 1 WLR 1212).

Planning and Preparation

Before executing a writ of possession against squatters or itinerants, the Officer must plan the operation with care. The object is to execute the warrant as soon as is reasonable and practical (*vide supra*), but without danger or injury to those involved. Executions of this type are potentially troublesome especially where they have been the subject of emotive press coverage and publicity.

Contact with the police must be established and, where necessary, their assistance requested. (See *post,* under ASSISTANCE). In consultation with the Under Sheriff and the police, the Officer must plan the eviction and to do so must be fully aware of the nature and geography of the premises or land and of the problems or interference that may be expected.

The Officer must keep in mind that every eviction, however insignificant or simple it may seem before the event, is potentially dangerous and he must pre-plan his action accordingly. Where a single Officer is instructed to execute such a writ, he must ensure that his immediate manager is aware of his location and expected action at all times and he should report to his manager immediately after the event. In the absence of such a report, the manager should raise such alarm as is necessary to ensure the Officer's safety.

The responsibility for the eviction rests with the Sheriff and the Officer but the responsibility for securing the premises afterwards is that of the landlord. When the premises have been cleared, the Officer should conduct the landlord's representative over the entire area to satisfy him that all persons have been removed. The warrant should then be endorsed by the landlord to the effect that possession has been given. An endorsement along the lines of, "Received vacant possession of the

within named premises this   day of   , 19 ", followed
by a signature is sufficient.

   The execution is at an end when possession has been
received by the landlord and the Sheriff has no right to
remain on the premises thereafter.

WRIT OF RESTITUTION

Where a person re-enters the premises after eviction, the
landlord cannot require the Sheriff to re-execute the writ
of possession. A writ of restitution is technically a writ
in aid of another writ of execution and leave to issue is
required. The Sheriff's return to the original writ should
be filed and then application can be made *ex parte* on an
affidavit of facts (RSC, O.46/3/2). The Master will order
the issue of a writ of restitution which may then be
executed in a like manner to the writ of possession. In the
case of a re-occupation of land after an eviction under
RSC, O.113, the Court will give leave to issue the writ,
even where the re-occupation is not by the same persons,
and indeed after a lengthy period of time, provided that
a sufficient link can be shown between the two events,
(*Wiltshire CC v. Frazer (No.2)* (1986) 1 WLR 109, 1 All
ER 65).

COMPULSORY PURCHASE ORDERS

The Police authorities take the view that the powers in
s.8 of the Sheriffs Act 1887 to call upon them as the *posse
comitatus* do not extend to the execution of a Compulsory
Purchase Order as that order is not a judicial writ but is
an administrative process.

   In such cases, a request for support by the police may

only be made to prevent a breach of the peace.

Otherwise, the execution is carried out in a similar manner to a judicial writ of possession. It should be noted however, that the warrant does not expire by the effluxion of time or by execution and may be executed more than once in the event of a reoccupation.

ASSISTANCE AND SUPPORT

The Sheriff's Act, 1887 states in s.8(2):

> "If a sheriff finds any resistance in the execution of a writ he shall take with him the power of the county, and shall go in proper person to do execution, and may arrest the resisters and commit them to prison, and every such resister shall be guilty of a misdemeanour."

It is therefore apparent that support and assistance may be used, on whatever scale is considered necessary, for the proper execution of the writ, but there has been considerable argument in the past as to the definition of "the sheriff ... in proper person". Opinions have been sought to establish whether this includes the Under Sheriff or the Sheriff's Officer, the final interpretation remaining undecided. If any prosecution under s.8 is to be guaranteed of success, the Sheriff himself should be present.

For the execution of normal writs, the presence of the police may be requested should the Officer fear a breach of the peace. The Officer would be entitled to expect the same protection and assistance as would be afforded to any member of the public who experienced interference in the conduct of their duty, and no more.

For the execution of warrants following writs issued

under RSC, O.113, there is the added protection of s.10, Criminal Law Act 1977 which states:

"(1) Without prejudice to s.8(2) of the Sheriffs Act 1887 but subject to the following provisions of this section, a person is guilty of an offence if he resists or intentionally obstructs any person who is in fact an Officer of a court engaged in executing any process issued by the High Court or any County Court for the purposes of enforcing any judgment or order for the recovery or for the delivery of possession of any premises."

(2) This restricts the above to Orders for possession where the occupancy was illegal: squatters, itinerants etc.

"(3) In any proceedings for an offence under this section it shall be a defence for the accused to prove that he believed that the person he was resisting or obstructing was not an officer of the court."

(4) Maximum penalty is six months imprisonment or £1000 or both.

"(5) A constable in uniform or any officer of a court may arrest without warrant anyone who is, or whom he, with reasonable cause, suspects to be, guilty of any offence under this section."

"(6) In this section 'officer of a court' means

(a) any sheriff, under sheriff, deputy sheriff, bailiff or officer of a sheriff; and

(b) any bailiff or other person who is an officer of a county court within the meaning of the County Court Act 1959."

In matters where the Officer anticipates serious problems,

he should consult with the Under Sheriff, in advance, as to whether it is advisable for the provisions of the Sheriffs Act to be used, in which event the Sheriff should be present in person, or whether the Criminal Law Act is considered to be more appropriate. If major difficulties are expected, the Under Sheriff must be involved throughout; it is the Under Sheriff who arranges the summoning of the *posse comitatus.*

Before proceeding under such warrants, there should be close liaison with the police and some agreement reached as to whether the Officer will make any arrests or whether it will be done by the constables present. As a matter of practicality, it is better for any prosecution to be conducted by the Crown Prosecution Service as they are more experienced in this field.

As it is a defence to prove that the Officer did not properly identify himself, care should be taken to ensure the occupants are in no doubt as to the Officer's authority. The warrant must be carried and produced if required, and the Officer may consider carrying a marking on his jacket, or an arm-band, indicating he is a Sheriff's Officer.

WRIT OF DELIVERY

The writ generally directs the Sheriff to put the plaintiff into physical possession of certain specified goods. The writ may be combined with a writ of *fi:fa* (RSC, O.45, r.4). The writ may be worded in the alternative, either to obtain payment of the assessed value of the goods or to obtain possession of the goods for the owner.

Where the writ so authorizes, the Sheriff should levy for the costs of executing the writ: the charges are the liability of, and are recoverable from, the debtor in the first instance by levy under the writ and not as in a writ of possession where they are the primary liability of the landlord. But in order to do so, the value of the goods must be known to be able to calculate the poundage due.

The warrant is executed in a like manner to a writ of *fi:fa*; entry may not be forced to residential premises (see *Mather*, 3rd Edn. p.194).

The normal practice is to arrange an appointment with the plaintiff to meet at the premises where the goods may be and for the Officer to "deliver" the goods specified. There are cases, particularly concerning motor vehicles, where it may be prudent for the Officer to take the goods into close custody as soon as they are found, giving delivery to the owner later. This course should not be taken without the knowledge and consent of the owner. The Officer should ensure that any removal and storage costs will be settled by the plaintiff. Costs appertaining to removal and storage are not costs of executing the warrant, they are costs which would have been incurred by the plaintiff once delivery had been given.

By analogy with a writ of possession, it is the duty of the plaintiff to identify or show the goods to be delivered.

Where it has proved impossible to execute a writ of delivery, or where the defendant has taken back the goods, either a writ of restitution or a writ of assistance may be issued in aid (see ch.13, LESS COMMON WRITS).

CHAPTER 13

Less Common Writs

In addition to writs of *fi:fa* and writs of possession, delivery and combinations of these, the Officer may be required to execute other less common writs. These are the writs of Assistance, *Venditioni Exponas* and *Ne Exeat Regno*. The first two are writs in aid of existing writs, the third a process on the way to final judgment.

By RSC, O.46, r.3, "A writ of execution in aid of any other writ of execution shall not be issued without leave of the Court." Specific leave of the Court is therefore necessary before any of these unusual writs are directed to the Sheriff. Application to the Court is usually made *ex parte* accompanied by an affidavit of the facts.

Writ of Assistance

This is issued where it has proved impossible, or will prove impractical to execute a normal writ of delivery or possession. As a writ of delivery is executed in a like manner to a writ of *fi:fa*, there is no authority to force entry to private premises, or to work the assets of the defendant and so on.

The authors have been informed that in the earlier part of the century, a writ of assistance was issued to allow an Officer to force open a safe where the plaintiff believed documents, the subject of the writ of delivery, were.

More recently, a writ of assistance was directed to the Sheriff of Greater London, to allow the Officer access to a computer to remove data from a data base and deliver it to the plaintiff, and then to delete that data from the computer memory (*Capscan Ltd v. Steiger Computers Ltd* (1984) unreported). The authors have also had the conduct of a writ of assistance in aid of a writ of possession where a mortgage defaulter continually re-entered the mortgaged premises after eviction.

The mode of execution of the writ will follow according to the directions it contains but in general it is unlikely to be completed in a simple manner. The writ will probably direct the Sheriff to enter the premises, with force if necessary, and to ensure that the plaintiff regains and retains peaceful use: "to maintain and keep him and his assigns in such peaceable and quiet possession ...", of the goods or land to be delivered. A writ of assistance may be directed to the "Present and future Sheriffs of ...", and in that case will not expire by the effluxion of time. Where a writ of assistance is issued in aid of a writ of possession or delivery, it may be executed as often as is necessary to keep the plaintiff in possession of the land or goods.

Venditioni Exponas

Leave to issue may be granted under RSC, O.46, r.3 where the Sheriff has made a return to the effect that no sale has taken place under a writ of *fi:fa* for want of buyers. The writ is a rarity, but has been issued within the past 25 years. The writ commands the Sheriff to, "expose to sale goods which he has already taken into his hands to satisfy a judgment creditor". In *Keighley v. Birch* (1814) 3 Camp 521, Lord Ellenborough defined the effect of the writ as being to, "sell for the best price you can obtain", and see also *Cameron v. Reynolds* (1776) Cowp 403.

The Sheriff must return the whole sum to the Court deducting nothing for extra expenses or poundage and the Court, when ordering his payment out of such sale proceeds, will allow him such poundage and costs on his motion (*Rex v. Jones* 1 Price 205).

Writ of *Ne Exeat Regno*

This writ, one of equitable bail, is issued prior to judgment and may only be sought when a creditor fears that the reputed debtor intends to leave the jurisdiction (Kingdom), with the prime object of avoiding judgment and the subsequent execution.

The warrant is directed by the Sheriff to, "The Keeper of the Gaol of the County and to My Bailiffs", and commands them to imprison the reputed debtor unless he pays to the Sheriff a sum certain as security. It is not surprising that there are few of these writs issued but at least two are known to the authors (*Buerex Securities Ltd v. Gilbert* (1976); *Mainchance Ltd v. Porcu & Others* (1985), both unreported).

On receipt of the writ, the Officer must ask the debtor to pay or to give sufficient security immediately for the sum required, failing which the debtor must be arrested and lodged in the gaol of the County. The writ does not allow the Officer to levy on the assets of the debtor. In view of the possible imprisonment of the debtor, the Officer must ensure that the instructing solicitors are kept fully informed as to the progress of the matter. On arrest and lodgment in prison, the warrant should be left with the gaoler as a detainer. For provisions and further practice regarding such arrests, see *Mather*, 3rd edn, at p.245 *et seq* and s.14, Sheriff's Act, 1887.

In *Al Nahkel for Contracting Trading Ltd v. Lowe* (1985) *Times Law Report*, December 21, Tudor Price, J declared that, although s.34(1) of the Prison Act, 1952 preserved the jurisdiction of the Sheriff in certain respects, he considered that there may be practical difficulties and that the writ of *ne exeat regno* was better executed by the Tipstaff who was not constrained by shrievalty boundaries. In view of this, future writs may well cease to be executed by the Sheriff although that particular judgment referred to an application for a writ in aid of a *Mareva* injunction.

The *Buerex* and *Mainchance* writs mentioned above both concerned matters where the debtors were believed to be leaving the jurisdiction before judgment could be obtained and neither were really concerned with a *Mareva* type application to the court. In *Mainchance*, the debtors were in fact a group of foreign holidaymakers who had rented a London flat for their holiday and were about to return home without paying the rental to the landlord.

CHAPTER 14

Sheriffs' Returns

The Purpose of a Sheriff's Return

A Sheriff's Return ("the Return") is a statement of how the writ of execution delivered to the Sheriff was executed. A creditor may need a return for various reasons. He may want to know that the execution has been completed and receive details of the amount recovered. He may want to use the information from the return as a basis to begin other means of enforcement, such as insolvency proceedings.

The Command for a Return

The writ addressed to the Sheriff will always contain the following command, referred to as the "endorsement" which states:

> "AND WE ALSO COMMAND YOU that you endorse on this writ immediately after execution thereof a statement of the manner in which you have executed it and send a copy of the statement to [name of the Plaintiff]."

This command is then passed by the Sheriff to the Officer

in the warrant as follows:

"AND I ALSO COMMAND YOU that immediately after the execution thereof you certify to me the manner in which you have executed this warrant."

Request for a Return

A party to the execution may send a notice to the Sheriff requesting a return. A fee of £5.00 plus VAT is payable (Sheriffs' Fees Amendment Order 1988). Generally the request is sent in the form of a letter, although the request may be prepared in the form of a short legal document (see Form No.1 in Appendix).

The Sheriff must give the return within the time stipulated in the notice (see RSC, O.46, r.9(1)). The time inserted in the notice to deal with the request is normally five days in London, and eight days elsewhere. The time may be extended on an application to the Court (see *Jones v. Robinson* (1843) 11 M & W 758).

Under RSC, O.46, r.9(1), either the judgment creditor or judgment debtor may apply to the Sheriff for a return. The return is usually requested after the execution has been completed. However, if there has only been a partial execution of the warrant, then a return can be made referring to this partial execution. A return in this form will not prevent the subsequent completion of the execution under the same writ (see *Lewis v. Holmes* (1847) 10 QB 896 and *Jordan v. Binckes* (1849) 13 QB 757).

Content of the Return

The return should state accurately the action taken by the Sheriff under the writ. Accuracy is important because the return may become part of an official record showing the action taken by the Sheriff under the writ. The recent case of *Re a Debtor* (No.340 of 1992), *The Debtor v. First National Commercial Bank plc and Another* [1994] 3 All ER 269 highlighted the need for an accurate statement of the action taken under the warrant. In that case a Sheriff made a return stating that the writ was "unsatisfied in whole". By virtue of s.268(1)(b) of the Insolvency Act 1986, where a return is given stating that the execution was "unsatisfied", the creditor is entitled to present a bankruptcy petition. In this case the Officer could not gain access to the debtor's house. The Court of Appeal held that s.268(1)(b):

> "contemplated the carrying out of execution and an endorsement of the manner in which execution was carried out. If the sheriff was unable to gain entry to the premises in which the execution was to be carried out, then there was no execution and a proper endorsement could not be made under the section."

Where the return is to be used to support insolvency proceedings, it should contain a statement that the execution remains unsatisfied in whole (or in part).

Signing the Return

The return is signed in the name of the High Sheriff and is normally attached to the original writ of execution delivered to the Under Sheriff. The "copy endorsement" (or copy form of return) is then sent to the party who has made the request.

False Return

A return which does not answer the command in the writ of execution, or is inaccurate, or false, may be set aside by the Court. A person who is injured by false information appearing in a return may bring an action against the Sheriff for a false return (see *Goubot v. De Crouy* (1833) 1 Cr & M 772). Malice on the part of the Sheriff need not be proved, although the injured party must prove actual damage (see *Brasyer v. McLean* (1875) LR 6 PC 398; *Wylie v. Birch* (1843) 4 QB 566).

Failure to Comply With Notice Requesting Return

If a Sheriff fails to respond to a request for a return, then the party who has asked for the information may apply to the Court to seek an order that the Sheriff complies with the request, (RSC, O.46, r.9(2)).

Action If the Writ is Lost

Even if a writ is lost (or mislaid), the Sheriff must be in a position to state what action has been taken under it (see *R. v. Sheriff of Kent* (1814) 1 Marsh 289). Provided proper records are kept of the action which has been taken, the loss of the original writ should not pose any problem to being able to make a proper return.

Intervening Insolvency

It is not necessary for the writ to be returned to be "complete" in terms of the Insolvency definition. Thus, in the case of intervening insolvency, the creditor may retain the proceeds of the execution that have been held for fourteen days regardless of whether or not the Sheriff has filed his return to the writ. (See *Re Hobson* (1886) 33 Ch D 493 and *Fulwood's Case* (1591) 4 Co Rep 64b at 67a). For forms of return where there is an intervening insolvency, see Forms 15 and 16 in the Appendix.

Invalid Writ of Execution

The Sheriff must make a return if requested to do so, even if the writ is found to be invalid (*Jones v. Williams* (1841) 8 M & W 349).

Pending Interpleader Proceedings

An execution creditor has no immediate right to a return if an interpleader issue is pending (*Angell v. Baddeley* (1877) 3 Ex D 49 CA).

A Return to One of Several Writs Held by the Sheriff

If asked to prepare a return to one of several writs held in his hands, the Sheriff should state in the return whether he has seized under that writ and should recite the details of the prior writs. "... and seizure by virtue of the several writs and according to the priority thereof" (see *Chambers v. Colman* (1841) 9 Dowl 588).

Special Bailiffs

Where the Sheriff has appointed a special bailiff at the request of the execution creditor, the creditor is not entitled to a return to the writ of execution. If the Sheriff receives a rule for a return in such a case, he should not make the return but move the Court to set aside the rule. If he returns the writ in the form "I appointed a Special Bailiff ..." the return may be set aside (see *Tait & Co. v. Mitchell* (1888) 22 LR Ir 327 and s.10(2), Sheriff's Act 1887).

Change of High Sheriff

For the period of six lunar months after ceasing to be in office, a Sheriff can be required to make a return, even if he has failed to transfer the writ for execution to the new Sheriff (see *R. v. Adderley* (1780) 2 Doug KB 463; *Yrath v. Hopkins* (1835) 2 Cr M & R 250 and Sheriffs Act 1887 s.28(3)). The incoming Sheriff cannot be called upon to make the return if the writ has not been transferred to him for execution (see *Holmes v. Elnitts* (1842) 6 Jur 994).

RETURNS TO COMMON WRITS OF EXECUTION

Returns for common writs of execution, ie, Writ of *fieri facias*, Writ of Possession and Writ of Delivery, can be summarized as follows:

Satisfied (Form 2)

Withdrawn from possession following instructions (Form 3)

Withdrawn from possession in view of third party claim (Form 4)

Withdrawn from possession following interpleader proceedings (Form 5)

Payment or sale of part - no other goods available for sale (Form 6)

Seizure under a prior writ of execution (Form 7)

Countermanded (Form 8)

Cannot gain admission to premises (Form 9)

No goods (*Nulla bona*) (Form 10)

Goods seized but unsold for want of buyers (Form 11)

Writ of possession (Form 12)

Writ of Possession and *fieri facias* (Form 13)

Writ of Delivery, no goods and none found (Form 14)

Writ of *fieri facias* - Seizure and delivery of goods to Official Receiver (Form 15)

Writ of *fieri facias* - Payment to Official Receiver of whole or part of the sum recovered (Form 16)

Return to a Writ of *Fieri Facias*

The writ of *fi:fa* commands the Sheriff to seize and sell the goods of the judgment debtor found within his bailiwick. A return to a fi:fa must state whether or not the debtor has goods within the county or bailiwick. A return to the effect that the debtor's house is barricaded so that the Sheriff cannot discover whether he has goods or not, is not a proper return and will be set aside (see *Munk v. Cass* (1841) 9 Dowl 332 and see also *Re a Debtor (No.340 of 1992), the Debtor v. First National Commercial Bank plc and Another* [1994] 3 All ER 269 referred to above).

The Return of "No Goods" (or a Return of *Nulla Bona*)

If the Sheriff cannot find any goods belonging to the judgment debtor then he will make a return of No Goods (or *nulla bona*). This return will not be appropriate where the debtor has goods (of whatever value) which can be applied to the present writ (see *Slade v. Hawley* (1845) 13 M and W 757).

A finding of "no goods" includes the following circumstances:

> where there are no goods at all belonging to the judgment debtor within the bailiwick;
> where the proceeds of sale of any goods which are found are insufficient to meet the costs of the levy;
> where there is a prior writ of execution;
> where there are other executions which enjoy Crown priority;
> where there is an unsatisfied claim by a landlord for outstanding rent under s.1 of the Landlord and Tenant Act 1709.

Goods Seized, but Unsold for Want of Buyers

If the Sheriff cannot attract a bid at auction for the goods seized, and has no offers for the goods in a sum approaching his valuation, then he will make a return in this form.

If a judgment creditor receives a return in this form but wishes the Sheriff to sell the remaining goods he may issue a Writ of *venditioni exponas* (for a return to this type of writ of execution see "Less Common Returns" set out below).

Return to a Writ of Possession

The return is subject to the general points appearing at the beginning of this chapter.

In giving possession the Sheriff will require the landowner or his representative to be present to receive possession of the land or property. That person will also point out the extent of the property covered by the Writ of Possession. If neither is present when the Sheriff attempts to execute the writ, and possession is not delivered to the landowner, this will be detailed in the return (*Floyd v. Bethill* (1616) 1 Roll Rep 420 and see Form 12 in the Appendix).

Return to a Writ of Delivery/Specific Delivery (RSC, O.45/4/2)

A return for a Writ of Delivery appears as Form 14 in the appendix.

LESS COMMON FORMS OF RETURN

Return to a Writ of *Venditioni Exponas*

The need for a writ of execution in this form has been set out above. It is a writ in aid of a Writ of *fieri facias* and is uncommon. A form of return for this type of writ appears in Form 17 in the appendix.

Return of No Goods and that the Defendant is a Beneficed Clerk

If a creditor wishes to execute a writ of *fieri facias* against the ecclesiastical goods of a rector or vicar of the Church of England ("referred to as a beneficed clergyman"), he must first obtain a return of No Goods (or *nulla bona* (see *Rabbits v. Woodward* (1869) 20 L.T 693,778)) from the Sheriff.

In making the return the Sheriff must certify that the judgment debtor is a beneficed clerk and has no lay fee. The Sheriff will need to make the necessary inquiries with the appropriate officers of the church before being able to make the return.

Once the judgment creditor has a return from the Sheriff he can issue a writ of *fieri facias de bonis ecclesiasticis* or of sequestration *de bonis ecclesiasticis* which is then delivered to the Bishop of the appropriate diocese to be executed (see RSC. O.47, r.5).

A form of return to be made by the Sheriff enabling the judgment creditor to issue the writ of execution appears in the appendix as Form 18.

APPENDIX

**FORM 1 -
NOTICE TO SHERIFF FOR COPY ENDORSEMENT ON
WRIT**

[Prepare Heading as for Writ of Execution]

To the Sheriff of [insert county or bailiwick]

I hereby give you notice that I require you within [five] days
to endorse on the writ of [insert type of writ eg, *fieri facias*]
issued by the Plaintiff in the above action and tested [insert
teste date] a statement of the manner in which you have
executed it and send me a copy of such statement.

Signed .... (Plaintiff's solicitors)

Reference Details :

DATED the   day of   19

FORM 2 -
SATISFIED - RETURN TO WRIT OF *FIERI FACIAS*

IN THE HIGH COURT OF JUSTICE
                                [insert action number]
[   ] DIVISION
B E T W E E N :

[insert name of Plaintiff]   Plaintiff

and

[insert name of Defendant]   Defendant

COPY OF ENDORSEMENT

In pursuance of the Rules of the Supreme Court (Revision) 1965
Order 46 Rule 9, it is hereby certified that the following is a
true copy of the endorsement on the Writ of Execution in this
Action:

I CERTIFY and RETURN that I have caused to be made of the
goods and chattels of the within named [insert name of
Defendant] in my bailiwick the sum by endorsement on this
Writ directed to be levied which sum of money I have paid to
the within named [insert name of Plaintiff]

Dated [insert date]   [insert name of
                                High Sheriff] SHERIFF

FORM 3 -
WITHDRAWN FROM POSSESSION FOLLOWING INSTRUCTIONS

[Prepare Heading as for Form 2]

I CERTIFY and RETURN that I caused to be seized divers goods and chattels of the within named [insert name of debtor] and kept them safely until I received an Order from Messrs [insert name of plaintiff's solicitors] Solicitors to the above named Plaintiff requiring me to quit possession of the said goods and chattels whereupon I quitted possession of the said goods and chattels.

[Conclude as for Form 2]

FORM 4 -
WITHDRAWN FROM POSSESSION IN VIEW OF THIRD PARTY CLAIM

[Prepare Heading as for Form 2]

I CERTIFY and RETURN that I caused to be seized divers goods and chattels of the within named [insert name of debtor] and kept them until I received an Order from Messrs [insert name of plaintiff's solicitors] Solicitors to the above named Plaintiff requiring me to quit possession of the said goods and chattels [a claim to the said goods and chattels having been received and admitted] whereupon I quitted possession of the said goods and chattels.

[Conclude as for Form 2]

FORM 5 -
WITHDRAWN FROM POSSESSION FOLLOWING INTERPLEADER PROCEEDINGS

[Prepare Heading as for Form 2]

I CERTIFY and RETURN that I caused to be seized divers goods and chattels of the within named [insert name of debtor] in my bailiwick and kept them which goods were afterwards claimed by [insert name of Claimant] as [his/her/their] goods and chattels

I FURTHER CERTIFY and RETURN that in obedience to an Interpleader Order made in respect of this claim by [insert name of Master or District Judge] [insert date of Order] the Sheriff was ordered to withdraw from possession of the said goods and chattels claimed whereupon I withdrew from possession of the said goods and chattels

[Conclude as for Form 2]

FORM 6 -
PAYMENT OF PART RECEIVED, NO FURTHER GOODS AVAILABLE FOR SALE

[Prepare Heading as for Form 2]

I CERTIFY and RETURN that I have caused to be made of the goods and chattels of the within named [insert name of debtor] to the value of £[insert value of goods seized] part thereof I have retained in my hands for poundage, Officers' fees, costs of levying and other expenses of the execution amounting to £ [insert amount retained] the residue whereof namely £[insert amount paid to plaintiff's solicitors] I have paid to Messrs [insert name of Plaintiff's Solicitors] Solicitors for the above named Plaintiff.

The said [insert name of debtor] has no other goods or chattels which I can levy against for the residue of the said monies or any part thereof.

[Conclude as for Form 2]

FORM 7 -
SEIZURE UNDER A PRIOR WRIT OF EXECUTION

[Prepare Heading as for Form 2]

I CERTIFY and RETURN that I caused to be seized divers goods and chattels of the within named [insert name of debtor] and kept them safely until I received an Order from Messrs [insert name of plaintiff's solicitors] Solicitors to the above named Plaintiff requiring me to quit possession of the said goods and chattels (there being prior writs of execution remaining unsatisfied) whereupon I quitted possession of the said goods and chattels.

[Conclude as for Form 2]

FORM 8 -
COUNTERMANDED WRIT OF EXECUTION

[Prepare Heading as for Form 2]

I CERTIFY and RETURN that pursuant to instructions from Messrs [insert name of plaintiff's solicitors] Solicitors for the above named Plaintiff I forbore to execute this Writ.

[Conclude as for Form 2]

FORM 9 -
CANNOT GAIN ADMISSION TO PREMISES

[Prepare Heading as for Form 2]

I CERTIFY and RETURN that despite attendances at [insert address] on [insert dates as appropriate] to levy on the goods and chattels of the within named [insert name of debtor] I have been unable to gain access to seize such goods and chattels.

I therefore return this Writ as being unsatisfied in whole of the monies within mentioned as I am within commanded

[Conclude as for Form 2]

FORM 10 -
NULLA BONA - No Goods

[Prepare Heading as for Form 2]

I CERTIFY and RETURN that the within named [insert name of debtor] has no goods or chattels in my Bailiwick whereof I can cause to be made the within mentioned monies or any part thereof.

I therefore return this Writ as being unsatisfied in whole.

[Conclude As in Form 2]

FORM 11 -
GOODS SEIZED BUT PART UNSOLD FOR WANT OF BUYERS

[Prepare Heading as for Form 2]

I CERTIFY and RETURN that I caused to be made of the goods and chattels in my bailiwick of the within named [insert name of debtor] to the value of £[insert net sum received] which money I have paid to the within named [insert name of Plaintiff] as I am within commanded and the residue of the said goods and chattels remain in my hands unsold for want of buyers.

[Conclude As in Form 2]

FORM 12 -
WRIT OF POSSESSION

[Prepare Heading as for Form 2]

I CERTIFY and RETURN that on the [insert date of execution of warrant] I caused the within named [insert name of plaintiff] to have possession of [insert address/area] with the appurtenances in my bailiwick as I am within commanded

[or alternatively, if no one came to point out the land or receive possession]

I certify and return that this writ was delivered to me on [insert date of delivery of Writ of Execution] since which time I have always been ready and willing to execute the same as within I am commanded but neither the within-named [insert name of Plaintiff] nor any person on his behalf ever came to show me the [land or premises] within mentioned or any part thereof or to receive possession of the same or any part thereof from me.

[Conclude As in Form 2]

FORM 13 -
WRIT OF POSSESSION AND *FIERI FACIAS*

[Prepare Heading as for Form 2]

I CERTIFY and RETURN that on [insert date of possession of premises] I caused the within-named [insert name of Plaintiff] to have possession of [insert description of premises] with the appurtenances in my bailiwick as I am within commanded.

I further certify and return that I have caused to be made of the goods and chattels of the within-named [insert name of debtor] in my bailiwick the sum by the endorsement of this writ directed to be levied, which sum of money I paid to the within-named [insert name of Plaintiff] in satisfaction of the money within mentioned as I am within commanded.

FORM 14 -
WRIT OF DELIVERY - NO GOODS and NONE FOUND

[Prepare Heading as for Form 2]

I CERTIFY and RETURN that the within named [insert name of debtor] has no goods or chattels in my bailiwick which I can seize or take or pay or deliver to the within named [insert name of plaintiff] or whereof I can cause to be made the monies mentioned in this Writ or any part thereof as I am commanded

[Conclude As in Form 2]

FORM 15 -
WRIT OF *FIERI FACIAS* - SEIZURE AND DELIVERY OF GOODS TO OFFICIAL RECEIVER

[Prepare Heading as for Form 2]

I CERTIFY and RETURN and by virtue of this writ directed to me I caused to be seized and taken in execution goods and chattels of the within-named [insert name of debtor] to the value of £[insert value of goods], and before the sale of those goods as I am commanded under the Writ of Execution, notice was served on me that a bankruptcy order dated [insert date of bankruptcy order] had been made by the [High Court of Justice or [   ] County Court] against the said [insert name of debtor], and I therefore delivered the said goods and chattels to the Official Receiver [insert name and address of Official Receiver], as named in the said order pursuant to Section 346 (2) of the Insolvency Act 1986, on [insert date of delivery to Official Receiver].

Therefore I cannot have that sum as I am within commanded.

[Conclude As in Form 2]

FORM 16 -
WRIT OF *FIERI FACIAS* - PAYMENT TO OFFICIAL RECEIVER OF WHOLE OR PART OF SUM RECOVERED

[Prepare Heading as for Form 2]

I CERTIFY and RETURN that by virtue of this writ to me directed I have caused to be made of the goods and chattels of the within-named [insert name of debtor] [or part of] the sum by the endorsement of this writ directed to be levied.

And I further certify that the said sum of £[insert amount of net proceeds] [being the whole of the proceeds of the sale of the goods and chattels of the said [insert name of debtor] in my bailiwick] came into my hands on [insert date of receipt] when the said goods were sold or was paid to me on [insert date of payment] in order to avoid a sale under this writ and that I then deducted from that sum £[insert amount deducted] for my costs of the execution and that while the balance of £[insert balance] was still in my hands, I was served on [insert date of service of bankruptcy notice] with notice that a bankruptcy petition had been presented [against or by] the said [insert name of debtor] to the [High Court of Justice or [insert name of court]County Court] in bankruptcy on which a bankruptcy order was made on [insert date of order], and pursuant to Section 346 (2) of the Insolvency Act 1986, I paid the said balance of £[insert balance] to the Official Receiver [insert name of Official Receiver] named in the said order.

Therefore I cannot have that sum as I am within commanded.

[Conclude As in Form 2]

FORM 17 -
RETURN FOR WRIT OF *VENDITIONI EXPONAS*

[Prepare Heading as for Form 2]

I CERTIFY and RETURN that by virtue of this writ directed to me I have sold the goods levied on for the amount directed and have the money in this Court to be rendered to the Plaintiff.

[Conclude As in Form 2]

FORM 18 -
RETURN TO WRIT OF *FIERI FACIAS* OF NO GOODS AND THAT DEFENDANT IS A BENEFICED CLERK

[Prepare Heading as for Form 2]

I CERTIFY and RETURN that the within-named [insert name of the debtor] has no goods or chattels nor any lay fee in my bailiwick which I can seize or take or pay or deliver to the within-named [insert name of plaintiff] or whereof I can cause to be made the sum by the endorsement of this writ directed to be levied or any part thereof as I am within commanded; but I do certify that the said [insert name of the debtor] is a beneficed clerk, namely [rector/vicar] of the [rectory/vicarage] and parish church of [name of church] in my county which said [rectory/vicarage] and parish church are [within the diocese of the Right Reverend Father in God [insert name of Bishop] by Divine permission Lord Bishop of [state diocese of Bishop] [or within the peculiar jurisdiction of the Very Reverend the Dean and Chapter of the Cathedral Church of St [insert as appropriate]] and instituted to try them as ordinary [or as the case may be].

[Conclude As in Form 2]

CHAPTER 15

Injunction and Stays of Execution

The execution of a warrant may be stopped or "stayed" as a result of a further order of the Court. Generally the defendant to the action will make an application to the Court to prevent the judgment against him being executed. The application may be made in stressful circumstances. The Sheriff, through his solicitors and Officers, must be able to respond to any order which is made, and the order must be obeyed immediately. If the Sheriff is unsure about the extent of the order, or is in any way uncertain about what to do, the matter should immediately be referred to the person who made the order, be it a Master, Judge or District Judge. Under no circumstances should the Officer or the Sheriff's solicitor take it upon themselves to interpret the terms of the order.

Stay of Execution

Once a judgment or order has been made the Court can only grant a stay of execution in limited circumstances. The power of the Court to grant a stay of execution will depend on the nature of the judgment. An application to have judgment set aside or varied is not a stay of execution. If such an application is made, then an application for a stay of execution pending the outcome of the application for judgment to be set aside or varied will also be necessary.

Often the order will be endorsed on the back of a summons or other court document and will be written by the Master, Judge or District Registrar. The order is effective from the moment it is made, and should be acted upon immediately. As the order will often be handwritten, it is worth taking a few moments to check the authenticity of the order and that it is fully understood. If any part of the order is unclear then the matter should be referred to the person who made it.

Staying Execution of a Writ of *Fieri Facias*

A judgment or order for the payment of money can be stayed either absolutely, or for such period and subject to such conditions as the Court thinks fit (see RSC, O.47, r.1(1)).

The usual form of order is that the execution of the writ of *fieri facias* will be stayed so long as the judgment debtor pays the amount of the debt and costs by specified instalments on specified dates, and, if he defaults in meeting any instalment on the due date, the stay will be removed for any outstanding balance.

Any order granting a stay may be varied or revoked by a subsequent order, (RSC, O.47, r.1(5)).

In cases of urgency where, for example perhaps the Sheriff's Officers are at the premises to remove goods, the debtor can attend before the Practice Master to seek a stay of execution pending the hearing of a summons. Stays obtained in these circumstances are usually very frantic affairs. The Sheriff is rarely represented at the hearing. It then falls upon the execution creditor to instruct the Sheriff so that the Sheriff obeys the order of the Court (see *Montague v. Davies Benachi & Co.* [1911] 2 KB 595).

Where a formal seizure of the goods has been made by the Sheriff, then any order made by the Court should clearly direct whether the Sheriff should withdraw from possession, and if so, when.

If the Officers and/or removal contractors are in the process of removing the goods from the debtor's premises, the removal should cease immediately. Goods which have been loaded on to the removal vehicle should be taken into store. Goods still remaining in the premises should remain in the premises. The object of this is to maintain the *status quo* at the time of the order coming to the knowledge of the Officer. If the debtor wishes the return of the goods already taken, he should seek a further and more specific order from the Court. As a precaution, and as a matter of good practice, the Officer should record accurately the time the stay was received and at what time the removal vehicle left the premises. Without such information the Officer can leave himself open to an accusation that the stay was not acted upon when it was received.

Frequently the Officer will be met with an order for a stay of execution following Interpleader Order No.1 where the claimant's claim is barred. Depending on when the stay is received, the Officer should act as set out in the previous paragraph. It is always open to a debtor or claimant to pay the amount due under the warrant and then make the appropriate application to the Court as to why the goods should be returned to them. Such a payment will prevent further removal and storage charges being incurred.

Stay of Execution Pending Appeal

The decision by an execution debtor to appeal a judgment or order should not be regarded as a stay of execution. The power to stay the execution of a *fi:fa* is quite separate and distinct from the power to stay execution pending an appeal (see *Ellis v. Scott* [1964] 2 All ER 987 and also RSC, O.59, r.13). Therefore if a debtor fails to apply for a stay of execution pending the appeal, any intermediate act, such as removal of the goods, will be valid.

Anton Pillar Order and Interaction with Execution

If a creditor believes a debtor will destroy material or documents which will lead to the discovery of assets, then the creditor may obtain an *Anton Pillar* order "in aid of the execution" (see *Distributori Automatici Italia SpA v. Holford General Trading Co. Limited* [1985] 3 All ER 750).

The order is similar to a form of "search warrant". Following the case of *Universal Thermosensors Limited v. Hibbern* [1992] 3 All ER 257 (which involved the execution of an *Anton Pillar* order at 7.15 am where only a woman and her children were in the house, and where the woman had no opportunity of obtaining legal advice), the granting and implementation of the order is strictly monitored by the Courts. The execution of the order must now be overseen by a "supervising solicitor".

It will be noted that the standard order provides that:

"it may only be served between 9.30 am and 5.30 pm on a week day". In addition, "the Defendant must allow (those persons who are serving the order) to remain on the premises until the search is complete and if necessary to re-enter the premises on the same or the following day in order to complete the search".

If the Officer is faced with such an order, he may find the effects are taken by the plaintiff for production to the Court. This should be permitted, subject to the seizure by the Sheriff. The effects are in a position similar to that of goods in the custody of the Police. The disposal of the effects may be determined on the outcome of the trial following the *Anton Pillar* order.

Mareva Injunction and Interaction with Execution

A creditor can use a *Mareva* Injunction (from the case *Mareva Compani Naviera SA v. International Bulk Carriers SA* [1975] 2 Lloyd's Rep 509) to prevent a debtor from disposing of his assets. It can be obtained at any time before or after judgment if it becomes apparent that the debtor is going to dispose of any goods to defeat the creditor. As the Officer is levying under a warrant issued after a judgment, any later writ of *fieri facias* issued by a party seeking a *Mareva* injunction would be subsequent in priority.

As with an *Anton Pillar* order, the granting and implementation of a *Mareva* injunction is strictly controlled by the Courts. It can only be used where:

(a)   the plaintiff has a good arguable case for an ascertained or a reasonably ascertainable sum; and

(b)   there is evidence that there is a real risk that assets which are currently available will not be available when judgment is obtained; and

(c)   it will be just and convenient in all the circumstances to grant the injunction.

A Sheriff may come "to the aid of *Mareva*" in the
following way:

The Sheriff has his duties under the writ and cannot
break into premises. But where a judgment creditor needs
to know the extent of the debtor's assets the Court has
been willing to make an order in the following form:

"That the defendant do permit the Sheriff of the county
of [insert name of county or bailiwick] his Officers,
servants or agents to enter upon the land and buildings
namely [description of land or buildings] for the
purpose only of taking an inventory of all chattels
personal".

In allowing entry into the premises in this way, although
the Sheriff can enter the premises, he cannot make a
formal seizure and is only entitled to compile an inventory
to be used as evidence of the debtor's assets. The Officers
must leave the premises as soon as the inventory is
completed.

CHAPTER 16

Sheriff's Fees

The Sheriff or his Officer may only demand and receive the fees and poundage prescribed in the Scale of Fees. He may not take or demand any reward for doing or abstaining from doing his duty or for any exertion he may make in the execution of a writ, no matter how arduous or unusual. (Sheriffs Act, 1887, s.20; *Slater v. Hames* (1841) 7 M & W 413).

Section 29(b), Sheriffs Act 1887 made it an offence for any Sheriff, Under Sheriff or Officer to take or demand any money or reward other than the fees allowable by statutory authority but that section was repealed on the passing of the Theft Act 1968. Such taking and demanding is now an offence under that Act.

An overcharge made from an innocent mistake does not make the Sheriff liable to penalties under the Sheriffs Act (or Theft Act, *supra*), (*Lee v. Dangar* (1892) 2 Q.B.237; *Shoppee v. Nathan* (1892) 1 QB 245), and delivering an account containing items which were greatly reduced on taxation is not a taking or demanding of money above the legal fees contrary to the statute, if the account is rendered in contemplation of taxation (*Woolford's Estate v. Levy* (1892) 1 QB 772).

The Sheriff may not take a bond for his fees and a Sheriff or Under Sheriff may not refuse to execute a writ or process until his fees have been paid. A promise to pay extra remuneration for execution of a process is void. Even though the Sheriff knows the creditor is "a man of straw", he may not refuse execution.

The Sheriff may sue the execution creditor for his fees if he is unable to recover them from the judgment debtor but this right does not extend to suing the creditor's solicitor except where a solicitor has interfered in an execution to the extent of making himself a party (*Royle v. Busby* (1881) 43 LT 717).

A Sheriff's Officer may not sue for fees due under an execution, he must leave them to be recovered by the Sheriff (*Smith v. Broadbent* (1892) 1 QB 551).

The Sheriff's Scales of Fees as amended to 1994

The Sheriff's Fees Order, 1920

This order concerns only the fees chargeable for the execution of a writ of *fi:fa*.

(VAT at the standard rate is to be added to all fees)

Mileage (Sheriff's Fees Amendment Order, 1988)

1(a) For mileage from the sheriff's officer's residence to the place of levy and return, in respect of one journey made to seize the goods and where appropriate one journey made to remove the goods   **per mile 29.2p**

1(b) Where the place of levy is distant more than one mile and a half from the nearest railway station, there may be allowed, in lieu of mileage from the station to the place, out of pocket expenses actually and reasonably incurred for the conveyance from the station to that place and back to the station.

This fee is payable only where there is in fact a seizure (*Townend v. Sheriff of Yorkshire* (1890) 24 QBD 621).

Seizure (Sheriff's Fees Amendment Order, 1971)

2. For seizure by the sheriff's officer for each building or place separately rated at which a seizure is made

£2.00

This fee is recoverable where a seizure is made but is not chargeable where a second writ was lodged directing the Sheriff to premises at which he was already in possession (*re Wells, ex parte Sheriff of Kent* (1893) 68 LT 231). However, where the Sheriff seized further goods under a subsequent execution, a second seizure fee has been allowed.

Inquiries

3. For work done by the Sheriff's Officer in making inquiries as to claims for rent or to goods where a claim in writing is received by the Sheriff's Officer, including copying claims and giving necessary notices to all parties, a sum not exceeding **£2.00**

and for all out of pocket expenses actually and reasonably incurred in relation to such work, including postage, telegraphic and telephonic messages, a further sum not exceeding **£2.00**

These fees are chargeable only where a written claim is received (3a) and submitted for instructions (3b). They are chargeable only once per warrant, not for each and every claim.

Possession (Sheriff's Fees Amendment Order, 1971)

   4. For keeping possession of goods and animals

   (a)   where a man is left in physical possession (the man in possession to provide his own board)
                                   per man per day £3.00

   (b)   where walking possession is taken under an agreement in the form set out in the Schedule to the Sheriff's Fees Amendment Order, 1956
                                   per day 25p

Note: This fee is payable in respect of the day on which the execution is levied but a fee for physical possession must not be charged where a walking possession agreement is signed at the time of levy.

The right to this fee accrues as soon as possession is taken but not where the execution is paid out or where goods are removed immediately or where the debtor requests immediate removal. It is only chargeable when possession is maintained, not after removal (*Grubb, ex parte Sims* (1877) 36 LT 340).

   The fee is only chargeable under one execution at a time, it is not chargeable simultaneously on successive executions (*Glasbrook v. David* (1905) 1 KB 615 CA).

   Possession money may not be recoverable from a Trustee in Bankruptcy if the possession was prolonged and unreasonable. The Sheriff may have to look to the creditor for re-imbursement (*re Beeston, ex parte Board of Trade* (1899) 1 QB 626; *re English and Ayling* (1903) 88 LT 127).

Removal and Storage

5. For the removal of goods or animals to a place of safe-keeping, when necessary, the sum actually and reasonably paid.

6. When goods or animals have been removed, for warehousing or taking charge of the same, the sum actually and reasonably paid.

7. For keep of animals while in the custody of the Sheriff, whether before or after removal, the sum actually and reasonably paid.

Note: No fees for keeping possession of goods or animals to be charged after the goods or animals have been removed.

For Sale or Preparation for Sale by Auction
(Sheriff's Fees Amendment Order, 1971)

8(1) When sale by auction takes place

(a)   Where the sale is held on the auctioneer's premises, for commission to the auctioneer, an inclusive charge to include all out of pocket expenses except costs of removal
On the first £100   **£15.00 per cent**

On the next £900   **£12.50 per cent**
Above £1000   **£10.00 per cent**

(b)   Where the sale is held on the debtor's premises, for commission to the auctioneer, in addition to out of pocket expenses actually and reasonably incurred, on the sum realized   **£7.50 per cent**

8(2) Where no sale takes place by auction or by private contract.

(a)   Where the goods have been removed to the auctioneer's premises, for commission to the auctioneer, an inclusive charge of **£10.00 per cent of the value** of the goods, to include all out of pocket expenses except costs of removal.

(b)   Where the goods have not been removed from the debtor's premises but work has been done by the auctioneer or the Sheriff's Officer with a view to sale, for his commission, in addition to out of pocket expenses actually and reasonably incurred, **£5.00 per cent of the value** of the goods.

This fee is to be charged only where the work done includes the preparation of a detailed inventory of the goods seized.

Difficulties will arise where the auctioneers seek a commission higher than that permitted (for example, specialist auctioneers dealing in fine arts, postage stamps, etc).

There is no provision in the scale for the insurance of the goods whilst on the auctioneer's premises, nor for the separate costs of advertising.

There is no provision in the scale for the Officer to

recover a fee for listing and valuing the goods, even if the work has been done, where the goods are subsequently sold by auction. There is no equivalent of the County Court appraisal fee. But where an inventory has been made for the purpose of interpleader proceedings, the charge may be made though the goods be sold subsequently.

Where no goods have been removed, the Officer may seek a charge for the valuation and inventory. Disputes may arise over that valuation. Parties to the execution may not appreciate that a valuation is an expression of opinion based on the experience of the valuer considering the purpose of the valuation, the market and demand at that specific time and the nature of the intended sale. The Officer should ensure this is explained and wherever possible indicate the basis and purpose of the valuation.

For Sale by Private Contract
(Sheriff's Fees Amendment Order, 1971)

9(a) **Half the percentage allowed on a sale by auction and in addition:**

(b) For work actually done in preparing inventory and valuation, and for all work (if any) actually done in preparing for sale by auction a sum not exceeding in any event **£2.50 per cent on the value** of the goods.

(c) And for advertising and giving publicity to any intended sale by auction, printing catalogues and bills and distributing and posting the same and for labour employed in lotting and showing the goods, the sums (if any), actually and reasonably paid.

A private sale may only take place after permission of the Court has been obtained.

Poundage (Sheriff's Fees Amendment Order, 1971)

10. Sheriff's poundage on the amount recovered, **£5** per cent up to £100 and **£2.50** per cent above that sum.

For further comments on poundage, see the later sub-chapter POUNDAGE.

Except where the judgment or order sought to be enforced is for less than £600 and does not entitle the plaintiff to costs against the person against whom the execution is issued, the foregoing fees numbered 1, 2, 3, 4, 5, 6, 7, 8(1), 9 and 10, shall be levied in every case in which an execution is completed by sale, as fees payable to sheriffs were levied before the making of this order.

In every case where execution is withdrawn, satisfied or stopped, the fees under this order shall be paid by the person issuing the execution, or the person at whose instance the sale is stopped, as the case may be.

The amount of any fees and charges payable under this table shall be taxed by a Master of the Supreme Court or a District Registrar of the High Court as the case may be, in case the sheriff and the party liable to pay such fees differ as to the amount thereof.

The remainder of the order concerned fees incurred before the making of the order.

The Sheriff's Fees Order 1921

This order concerns charges under other writs and matters dealt with by the Sheriff.

For Executing a Writ of Possession or Delivery

> To the bailiffs for executing warrants of *ne exeat* ......, writ of possession, ... and other like matters for each, if the distance from the Sheriff's office or the bailiff's residence does not exceed five miles   **£1.05**
> If beyond that distance, per mile   **2.5p**

This fee was incorporated in the scale which was made by order under the Sheriff's Act 1837 as amended by Order of May 2, 1921 and not altered or removed by the Order of 1971. In the 1993 edition of the Supreme Court Practice it is suggested that it is no longer applicable yet it does remain. It appears to have been overlooked in the drafting of the 1971 Order.
The fee is chargeable for each Officer attending.

Lodgment (Sheriff's Fees Amendment Order, 1971)

> For every warrant which shall be granted by the Sheriff to his Officers upon any writ or process (other than at the suit of the Crown)   **£2.00**

Again the 1993 edition of the Supreme Court Practice fails to make reference to this fee.

7(a) **Mileage** (Sheriff's Fees Amendment Order, 1988)

For mileage from the Sheriff's Officer's place of residence to the place where the land or goods are situated and return, in respect of one journey made to execute a writ of possession or delivery   **per mile 29.2p**

Poundage, Possession (Sheriff's Fees Amendment Order, 1992)

7B(1) For executing a writ of possession of domestic property within the meaning of s.66 of the Local Government Finance Act 1988 poundage at the rate of **3** per cent of the net annual value for rating shown on the valuation list in force immediately before April 1, 1990 in respect of the property seized, subject to para.(3).

(2) For executing a writ of possession of property to which para.(1) does not apply, **0.4** per cent of the net annual value for rating of the property seized, subject to para.(4).

(3) For the purposes of para.(1), where the property does not consist of one or more hereditament which, immediately before April 1, 1990

    (a)   had a separate net annual value for rating shown on the valuation list then in force and

    (b)   was domestic property within the meaning of s.66 of the Local Government Finance Act 1988

the property or such part of it as does not so consist shall be taken to have had such a value for rating equal to two fifteenths of its value by the year when seized.

(4) For the purposes of para.(2), where the property does not consist of one or more hereditament having a separate net annual value for rating, the property or such part of it as does not so consist shall be taken to have such a value equal to its value by the year.

Poundage, Delivery (Sheriff's Fees Amendment Order 1971)

7(c) For executing a writ of delivery, poundage at the rate of £4.00 per cent of the value of the goods as stated in the writ of summons or judgment.

Returns (Sheriff's Fees Amendment Order 1988)

8. For a copy of any return by the Sheriff on a writ of execution   **£5.00**

Generally

9. For any duty not otherwise provided for, such sums as one of the Masters of the Supreme Court, or District Registrars of the High Court may upon special application allow.

Any fee or poundage to be charged under the Order of 1920 or the Order of 1921 or under either of those orders as amended by this Order, at the rate of 2.5 per cent, 7.5 per cent or 12.5 per cent on any sum shall be calculated on every £2.00 or part thereof of that sum.

Taxation provisions (Sheriff's Fees (Amendment) Order, 1992)

> The amount of any fees and charges payable under this Table shall be taxed by a Master of the Supreme Court or a District Judge of the High Court, as the case may be, in case the Sheriff and the party liable to pay such fees differ as to the amount thereof.

The scale does not provide for the hire of specialized transport and equipment required for the eviction of squatters, itinerants etc. It is wise therefore to ensure that the landlord provides these items or services.

VAT on Fees (Sheriff's Fees (Amendment) Order No.2, 1977)

Liability for VAT on the charges of the Sheriff arose from the provisions of the Finance Act, 1972, s.45 (4) and the schedule to the Finance Act, 1977, no.6 para.13, brought into force on January 1, 1978.

The Order (SI 1977 No.211) provided that, "where Value Added Tax is chargeable in respect of any service for which a fee is prescribed there shall be payable in addition to that fee the amount of the Value Added Tax".

The Customs and Excise advice dated 1992, in confirmation of their earlier 1978 statement and restated in 1994 said:

> "Sheriff's Officers and other people connected with the recovery of debt are normally regarded as office holders for VAT purposes and apart from the High Sheriff, their services are normally liable to VAT at the standard rate. High Sheriffs are appointed by the Crown and are not seen as accepting their office in the course or furtherance of a trade, profession or vocation."

"All supplies are made to the High Sheriff and as he is not receiving these supplies for the purpose of any business carried on by him, he will not be entitled to deduct input tax and hence will not require tax invoices to support a claim for such deduction. It should be noted that while debtors and creditors may be bearing the cost of the services, they are not the recipients of any of the supplies and cannot, if they are registered, deduct any of the VAT as their input tax."

"None of the persons in the enforcement process is required to issue tax invoices and any documents they issue to debtor or creditor should preferably not show the VAT separately. The document should be endorsed clearly 'All Sheriff's fees shown on this statement include VAT where chargeable, this is NOT a VAT invoice'. Each taxable person in the enforcement process, must, however, keep proper records of his supplies of services in accordance with Section X of Public Notice No.700. (August 1, 1991)."

It should be noted that all Sheriff's charges are liable to VAT (provided the Officer is a registered person for VAT purposes) regardless of the domicile of the creditor, foreign or otherwise.

POUNDAGE

Poundage is recoverable under warrants which are satisfied or are deemed to be satisfied or where monies are paid under pressure of the writ. It is the definition of "deemed to be satisfied" which will result in difficulties.

Mather on Sheriff and Execution Law states at p.608:

> "The fact that there has actually been a sale of the judgment debtor's goods is not the exclusive test of the right of the Sheriff to poundage. It is sufficient if there has been a seizure and the money is obtained either directly or indirectly."

The majority of queries and comments which will be made will be of a legal rather than a practical nature and will be best answered by the Under Sheriff to whom the Officer should look for direction. However, as the Officer will be placed in the position of having to quote charges before the queries are raised, it would be beneficial to consider certain basic aspects.

The authors are grateful to the former Under Sheriff of Greater London, Alastair Black, Esq, CBE, DL, for his permission to reproduce an article contained in the January 1979 edition of the Journal of the Sheriffs' Officers' Association.

> "There have been a number of decided cases on the Sheriff's charge to poundage, none of which I admit, are 'modern' but my firm has had the benefit of correspondence over the years with solicitors, liquidators, the Official Receiver, etc, as to the interpretation of the rules governing this charge. Further we also have experience of taxation of Sheriff's charges before the Taxing Master.
>
> "I would suggest, with respect, that the present understanding of the Law is as follows:
>
> "1.   Where a sale of the debtor's goods takes place, clearly there is no difficulty whatsoever and poundage is charged on the amount realised by

the sale.

"2.   Difficulties begin to arise where no sale of goods takes place. As Cave, J said at p.417 in *re Ludmore (or Ludford)*, (1884) 13 QB 415:

> 'where goods are not sold there would be very great difficulty in ascertaining what amount of poundage the Sheriff was entitled to, because poundage is a percentage, or commission on the amount obtained by sale.'

"In circumstances where no sale takes place, the Sheriff is entitled to charge poundage on the amount endorsed on the writ of *fi:fa* if he has seized goods under the writ and (a) the debtor (or a third party on his behalf) pays out the debt or (b) the creditor withdraws the Sheriff on finalising terms with the debtor. Obviously, goods may be of greater value to a debtor than the sale price that would be obtained by a forced sale by public auction and he may pay more to protect them rather than allow the goods to go for sale.

"The right of the Sheriff to charge poundage where no sale takes place was recognized in 1899 in *Re Thomas v. Sheriff of Middlesex* (1899) 1 QB 400 where Lindley, MR at p.462 said:

'The Sheriff has seized no doubt but he has not sold. It has been law settled for years that he is not entitled to poundage. I am aware that there has been a qualification on that where the Sheriff has seized, but has not sold in consequence of a compromise between the parties; there the law regards him as having secured the money for the creditor and gives him poundage. The 'qualification' mentioned by Lord Lindley had already been used by Lord Ellenborough to include poundage to the Sheriff on money obtained where the judgment has subsequently been set aside; *Bullen v. Ansley* (1807) 6 ESP 111. The Sheriff having regularly levied under the authority of the writ of execution has nothing to do with the regularity or irregularity of the proceedings under which the writ had been issued, this was an act of the party himself, by whom it was sued out, the authority of the writ the Sheriff could not question, but was bound to obey. He had therefore paid proper obedience to the writ and a statute having given him certain fees for his trouble as poundage, he was legally entitled to those fees on account of his levy.'

"*Madley v. Greenwood* (1897) 42 SJ 34 is also support for this argument. In that case, where the execution creditor's solicitors stopped the sale of sufficient goods to satisfy the writ, the Divisional Court allowed the Sheriff of Staffordshire's appeal and directed the Registrar to tax poundage which he had previously refused to do as the Sheriff had not actually handled the money. The case does not however go on to deal with what actually happened on the taxation of poundage when it took place!

"I would also draw your attention to the case of *Mills v. Harris* (1862) 13 CB (ns) 550 per Willis, J at p.559:

'I think the distinction is this - Where the execution has been regularly conducted and the Sheriff has levied the money under it, he is entitled to his poundage, though the judgment may afterwards be set aside for irregularity, for he has done all that he was required by the writ and warrant to do; so, where the Sheriff is ready to perfect the levy by sale and the parties compromise the Sheriff in consequence withdraws, for in that case the plaintiff has had all the benefit of the Sheriff's services and the Sheriff has done all that he could do, and was ready to do the rest in obedience to the precept, and according to all ordinary principles he ought to be paid.'

"The general statement of liability to the execution creditor is as stated by Phillimore, LJ in *Montague v. Davies Benachi & Co.* (1911) 2 KB 595:

'From the time of Elizabeth onwards it has been settled law that the execution creditor who puts the Sheriff in motion is liable to the Sheriff for his fees. If he withdraws an execution against goods under a *fi:fa*; or if the goods are not of sufficient value to cover the Sheriff's fees and charges, the execution creditor has to bear the loss.'

"Where the execution creditor withdraws the Sheriff under an instalment arrangement with the debtor, whereby the debtor has agreed to pay the debt by instalments, the Sheriff is entitled to charge poundage as on a fructuous execution and the poundage charged would be on the amount of the writ of *fi:fa*. The test is 'Was the execution settlement achieved under the compulsion of the writ in the Sheriff's hands?'"

Satisfied

Where all the monies are recovered, and where those

monies are paid after action under the writ of *fi:fa*, poundage should be recovered on the amount of the levy, that is the debt, costs, costs of execution and interest.

Withdrawn on terms

With the increasing face value of writs, many matters are withdrawn following negotiations between the parties. In such cases, the Sheriff will expect to be paid poundage as he is prevented from proceeding. Hence the expression "deemed to be satisfied".

Mather on Sheriff and Execution Law states at p.608:

> "As to a compromise between the parties before sale, in *Alchin v. Wells* (1793) 5 TR 470, the plaintiff, having obtained a judgment, sued out a writ of *fi:fa* and delivered it to the Sheriff, who levied on the defendant's goods; after the Sheriff had been in possession for two days the plaintiff and the defendant compromised before the Sheriff sold any of the defendant's goods. It was held that the Sheriff was unquestionably entitled to poundage."

However, in many instances the terms of the arrangement between the parties should be considered when deciding the basis on which poundage should be charged, particularly where the value of the goods seized is considerably less than the amount of the execution.

If there is doubt in the mind of the Officer, he should consult with the Under Sheriff before quoting the fees due.

Judgment Set Aside

Where the judgment is set aside, the actions taken under the *fi:fa* are effectively set aside also (although the Sheriff is protected by the writ for any action he took under it). If monies have been recovered and are to be refunded to the debtor, the poundage should be restricted to that due on those monies only and will be payable by the creditor unless the Court orders otherwise.

If the judgment is set aside as to part, the value of the *fi:fa* is reduced to that of the monies still due. The Sheriff's charges are then based on that lesser figure unless more than sufficient monies had been received prior to the making of the Order.

Partially Abortive

If monies are received but the Officer fails to receive the residue, for example, following the submission of a third party claim, poundage is payable only on the actual sum recovered.

Sale

Poundage should be charged on the result of the sale together with any payments made by the debtor, up to the extent of the *fi:fa*. In the case where sufficient goods have been sold to satisfy rent claimed by the landlord and the execution or some part of it, poundage is also receivable on the monies recovered for the rent.

Writ of Possession

Poundage should be charged on the net annual rateable value of the premises or land forming the subject of the writ. It is necessary to determine whether the premises are domestic or commercial property in order to decide the proper rate of charge. In the case of domestic property which was in existence before April 1, 1990, the charge will be 3 per cent of the rateable value at that time. Commercial property will be charged at 0.4 per cent of the current value for Council Tax.

In the case of domestic property built after 1990 or having no rateable value, the correct basis will be 3 per cent of two fifteenths of its net (rental) value by the year (in effect 0.4 per cent). Commercial property having no established rateable value will be charged at the rate of 0.4 per cent of its net annual (rental) value. Where the property comprises both types, the charge should be calculated as a composite.

During the past decade, there have been writs of possession issued which appear to cover an entire site, such as a University or a forest, but possession was given in respect of part of the land only. If the Officer is not required to give possession of the whole and a global writ was obtained purely in case a further area was occupied, it may be prudent to agree a proportion of the rateable value.

Where there is no readily available rateable value, poundage should be charged on the current commercial annual rental of the premises or land. This is frequently open to doubt and a compromise should be reached with the owners. One example of such a compromise is the assessment of waste ground according to the number of caravans assuming a rental of, say, £x per caravan per week.

Writs of Delivery

Poundage should be charged on the value of the goods delivered. This may be known in advance of the execution but it is more common to await the disposal of the goods by the plaintiff before charging. Where goods are not to be sold after delivery an agreement must be reached as to value. This is particularly difficult when executing against documents, files etc. However, the value of the goods subject to the writ should be stated in the original pleadings or summons.

Lands Clauses Warrants

There is no separate scale of fees for warrants of this type. It is usual to seek fees as though the warrant were a writ of possession.

Appendices

The Supreme Court Act, 1981
as amended by the Statute Law (Repeals) Act, 1989
and the Courts & Legal Services Act, 1990

Section 138

138(1) Subject to subs.(2), a writ of *fieri facias* or other writ of execution against goods issued from the High Court shall bind the property in the goods of the execution debtor as from the time when the writ is delivered to the sheriff to be executed.

(2) Such a writ shall not prejudice the title to any goods of the execution debtor acquired by a person in good faith and for valuable consideration unless he had, at the time when he acquired his title

> (a)   notice that that writ or any other such writ by virtue of which the goods of the execution debtor might be seized or attached had been delivered to and remained unexecuted in the hands of the sheriff; or
>
> (b)   notice that an application for the issue of a warrant of execution against the goods of the execution debtor had been made to the registrar of a county court and that the warrant issued on the application either
>
>> (i)   remained unexecuted in the hands of the registrar of the court from which it was issued; or
>>
>> (ii)   had been sent for execution to, and received by, the registrar of another county court, and remained unexecuted in the hands of the registrar of that court.

(3) For the better manifestation of the time mentioned in subs.(1), it shall be the duty of the sheriff (without fee) on receipt of any such writ as is there mentioned to endorse on its back the hour, day, month and year when he received it.

246

(3A) Every sheriff or officer executing any writ of execution issued from the High Court against the goods of any person may by virtue of it seize

(a) any of that person's goods except

(i) such tools, books, vehicles and other items of equipment as are necessary to that person for use personally by him in his employment, business or vocation;

(ii) such clothing, bedding, furniture, household equipment and provisions as are necessary for satisfying the basic domestic needs of that person and his family; and

(b) any money, banknotes, bills of exchange, promissory notes, bonds, specialities or securities for money belonging to that person.

(4) For the purposes of this section

(a) "property" means the general property in goods, and not merely a special property;

(b) "sheriff" includes any officer charged with the enforcement of a writ of execution;

(c) any reference to the goods of the execution debtor includes a reference to anything else of his that may lawfully be seized in execution; and

(d) a thing shall be treated as done in good faith if it is in fact done honestly, whether it is done negligently or not.

Section 138A

138A (1) Where any goods seized under a writ of execution issued from the High Court are to be sold for a sum exceeding £20 (including legal incidental expenses), the sale shall, unless the court otherwise orders, be made by public auction, and not by bill of sale or private contract, and shall be publicly advertised by the sheriff on, and during three days preceding, the day of sale.

(2) Where any goods are seized under a writ of execution issued from the High Court and the sheriff has notice of another execution or other executions, the court shall not consider an application for leave to sell privately until the prescribed notice has been given to the other execution creditor or creditors, who may appear before the court and be heard on the application.

Section 138B

138B (1) Where any goods in the possession of an execution debtor at the time of seizure by a sheriff or other officer charged with the enforcement of a writ of execution issued from the High Court are sold by the sheriff or other officer without any claims having been made to them

    (a)   the purchaser of the goods so sold shall acquire a good title to those goods; and

    (b)   no person shall be entitled to recover against the sheriff or other officer, or anyone lawfully acting under his authority, for any sale of the goods or for paying over the proceeds prior to the receipt of a claim to the goods,

unless it is proved that the person from whom recovery is sought had notice, or might by making reasonable inquiry have ascertained, that the goods were not the property of the execution debtor.

(2) Nothing in this section shall effect the right of any lawful claimant (that is to say, any person who proves that at the time of sale he had a title to any goods so seized and sold) to any remedy to which he may be entitled against any person other than the sheriff or other officer.

(3) The provisions of this section have effect subject to those of ss.183, 184 and 346 of the Insolvency Act 1986.

Relevant Rules of the Supreme Court

Note: References are to Supreme Court Practice 1995

Relevant Rules of the County Court

References unless stated otherwise are to the
County Court Act 1984

Administration Order	Attachment of Earnings Act 1971 s.4
	CC Rules 1981 O.39, r.1 *et seq*
Appeals	s.81
Assaulting an Officer	s.14
Distress by Landlord	s.116
EEC Judgments	Civil Jurisdiction and Judgments
	Act 1982, sch.1
Enforcement of Fines	Magistrates Courts Act 1980, s.87
Enforcement of Legal Aid	Legal Aid Act 1974, s.35
Execution against goods	Part V
Issue a warrant	s.85
Time the warrant	s.85
Assistance of a constable	s.85
Protection of armed forces from execution	note to s.85
Priority of warrants	s.99
Erroneously setting aside	ditto
Instalments	s.86
Stay of Execution	s.88
Goods seizable	s.89
Forcing entry	note to s.89
Walking possession	ditto
Inventory following removal	s.90
	CC Rules 1981, O.26, r.12
Report after sale to debtor	ditto r.13
Rescue of goods, penalty	s.92
Delay before sale	s.93
Brokers and appraisers	ss.94/95
Sales by auction	s.97
Sales by Private Treaty	CC Rules 1981, O.26, r.15
Sale of third parties' goods	s.98
Insolvency Act 1986	note to s.98
Claim to goods	s.99 *et seq*
Interpleader	s.101
	CC Rules 1981, O.33, r.1 *et seq*
Rent Outstanding	s.102

Notes derive from County Court Practice 1994

Insolvency Rules 1986
(SI 1986 No. 1925)

Companies

Fees payable, voluntary arrangement   1.28(1B)
Any fees, costs, charges or expenses which -

> "would be payable or correspond to those which would be payable, in an administration or winding-up."

Advertisement of Administration Order   2.10

Advertisement of appt. of admin. rec.   3.2
    (Does not include reference to Sheriff)

Liquidator to pay expenses of O.R   4.107

Loss of qualification as practitioner   4.134
                                       136
Payment of Costs from assets   4.218

Individuals

Fees payable under Vol. Arrangement   5.28

> "The fees, costs, charges and expenses that may be incurred for any purposes of the voluntary arrangement are - Any fees, costs, charges or expenses which ..... would be payable or correspond to those which would be payable in the debtor's bankruptcy."

General
Costs of the Sheriff may be taxed   7.36

Insolvency (Amendment) Rules 1987
(SI 1987 No. 1919)

Application for Administration Order, Sheriff to be served with notice
of petition   2.6A

Companies

Individuals

Index